# BULLETPROOF®

# MONK

When the enemy is all around you –
and guns are pointed at your head –
the hardest path to follow – is your own.

The Bulletproof Monk is a mythical hero in a
modern world. He is here to teach people to
believe in themselves against overwhelming
adversity. Once again, a person must fight to
discover the right thing to do and fight even
harder to get it done.

That's why I'm excited to put this great story,
"Bulletproof Monk," onto the big screen. For
one, because it explores my two favorite
subjects: love and sacrifice. But also because
it's told through mind-blowing action. In my
movies, the hero must conquer his own inner
battle between good and evil before he can
win the outward battle with the "real" enemy.

Kar is a kid living in a violent world; he
knows he has a mission, but he doesn't know
how he can fulfill it. The Bulletproof Monk
has mastered his body, mind and soul. He
can catch a bullet with one hand while
caressing a butterfly with the other. He
understands that the world is in desperate
need of a hero, and so he becomes one –
without fear.

Kar is on a path where battlement and
destruction are part of the scenery. He can
sense danger, out-smart the most conniving
traitors and smash a room of armed men
with his martial artistry. But he also has
much to learn and it is only through life and
death trials that he will be able to find his
own strength and belief in himself.

I have been on this quest all my life and,
through movies, I fight these same inner
battles. I believe the skill of one's hands is
only as good as the honor in one's heart.
It really is a universal struggle that we all
must conquer. This is why this story makes
not only a great comic book but also a
profound and exciting film.

John Woo

As far as years go for the world, 1941 probably can be judged as not a very good one. Villains were aplenty and heroes were hard to come by. By June of that year, the Nazis were moving toward their final offensive on the Eastern front in the Soviet Union. Already, they had overrun much of Europe, including the invasion of Paris, the intense aerial bombardment of Britain, and the subjugation of Austria, Poland, Denmark, and Norway. With Britain weary from attack, the Soviet Union severely weakened from years of solely combating Germany's fascist forces on the Eastern front, and the U.S. still staunchly maintaining its "isolationist" posture, things for the most part looked well, pretty bad.

The Nazi infiltration and expansion throughout Europe on both the Eastern and Western fronts were part of Adolph Hitler's plan to consolidate power and establish Germany as a true Global Super Power. Hitler's philosophy was primarily founded on his intent to ethnically cleanse Europe of all non-Aryans, including Jews, Gypsies, Catholics, and many other ethnic minorities. Hitler's radical quest revolved around the notion of a glorious new society populated solely by the Aryan race, which he understood as naturally superior to all others.

The truth is that Hitler proved to be as erroneous as he was cruel. His search for the perfect Aryan quickly led him out of Germany since the original Aryans were not of pure Caucasian descent and not indigenous to his beloved Germany. Still convinced of his dubious assumption of the Aryan race as ultimately superior, he mobilized a search to the East for the origins of the Aryan gene.

He went about this task quietly. For this principle problem, the fact that the "great Aryans" didn't even originate in Europe, nipped at the heels of his very ideology and his master plan. Hitler quietly assembled a small group of SS scientists granted the title of "Ancestral Research Units" and deployed them on a mission to the East, including Tibet, to search out the pure genetic origins of the Aryans. And therein lies the starting point for our tale – Bulletproof Monk.

What Hitler's exact plan was, is not entirely clear. But the notion of searching for genetic material has led some scholars to suggest that genetic engineering may have been part of some diabolical plan. Now with Bulletproof Monk, we're not here to teach you history – so we've broken off a tale that takes liberties and is definitely a departure into fiction. But the truth is, the original story proves to be as dramatic as any one that any of us could have dreamt up. And we haven't lost sight of what our original point was – to demonstrate that from the ashes of destruction and tragedy are the seeds for creation. Bulletproof Monk is our version of the next generation of mythology and spirituality – showing us that truth and wisdom and spirit endure through the most horrible of times.

Gotham Chopra, Story Editor

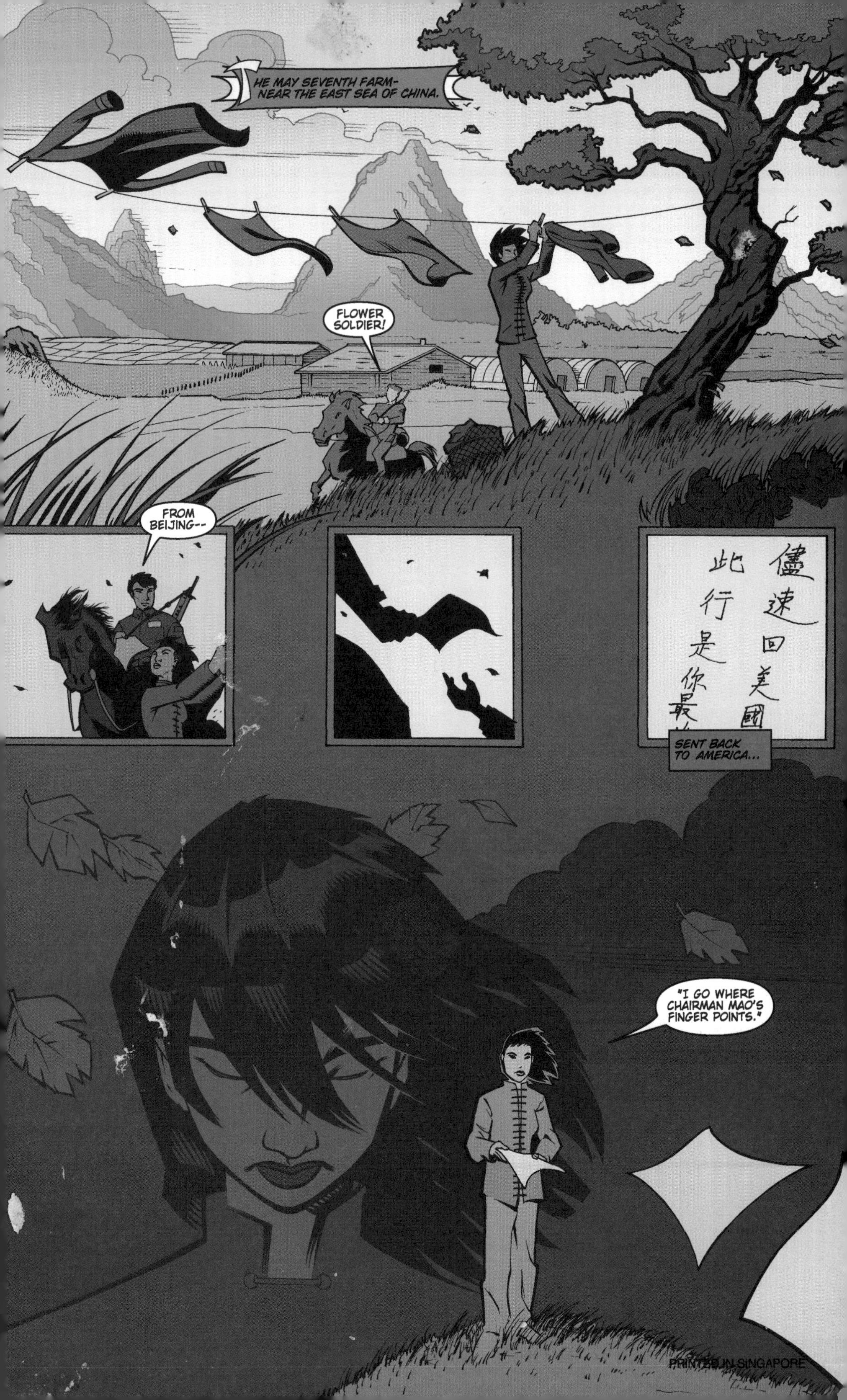
THE MAY SEVENTH FARM-
NEAR THE EAST SEA OF CHINA.
FLOWER SOLDIER!
FROM BEIJING--
儘速回美國
此行是你最
SENT BACK TO AMERICA...
"I GO WHERE CHAIRMAN MAO'S FINGER POINTS."

PRINTED IN SINGAPORE

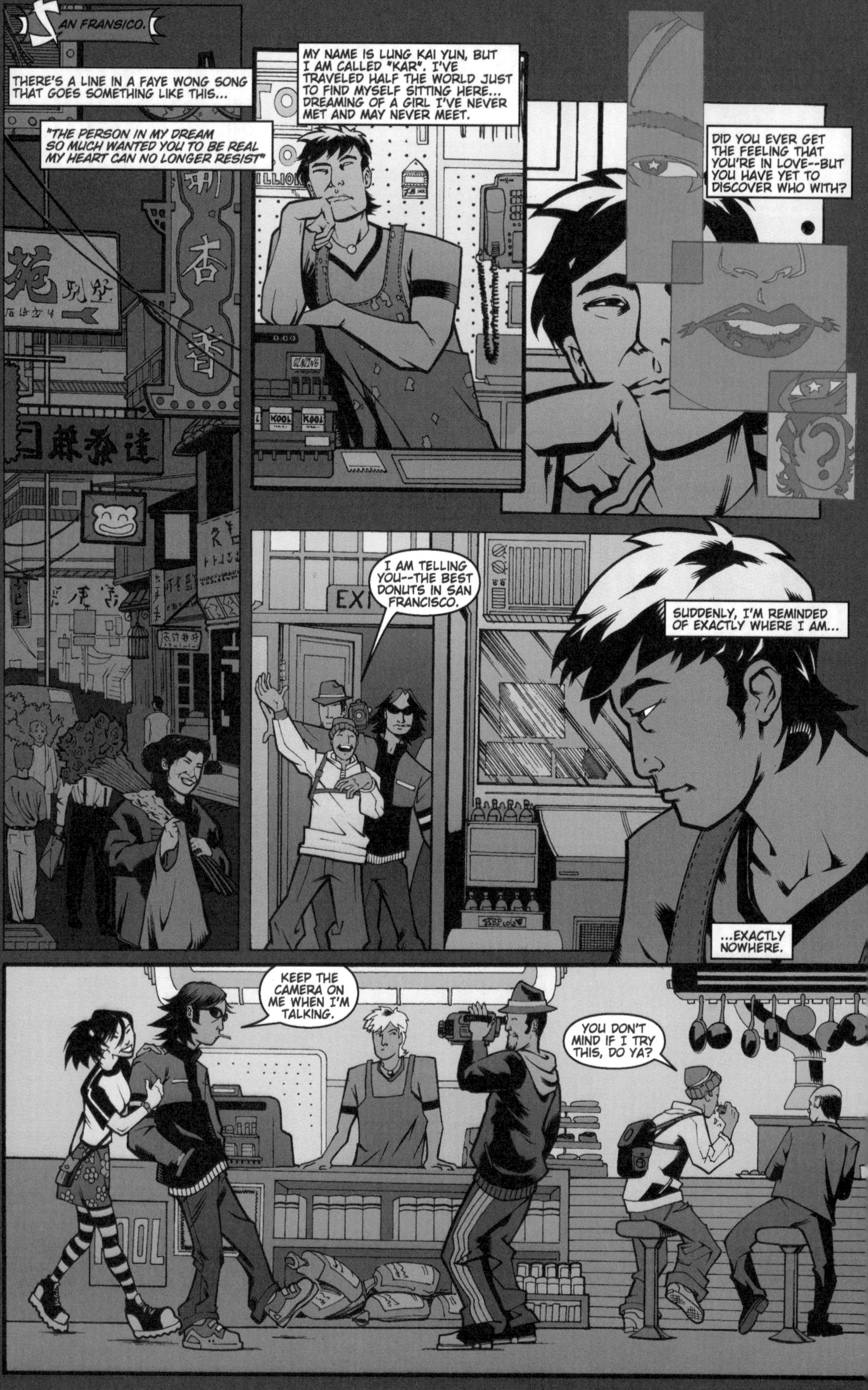
SAN FRANSICO.
THERE'S A LINE IN A FAYE WONG SONG THAT GOES SOMETHING LIKE THIS...
"THE PERSON IN MY DREAM SO MUCH WANTED YOU TO BE REAL MY HEART CAN NO LONGER RESIST"
MY NAME IS LUNG KAI YUN, BUT I AM CALLED "KAR". I'VE TRAVELED HALF THE WORLD JUST TO FIND MYSELF SITTING HERE... DREAMING OF A GIRL I'VE NEVER MET AND MAY NEVER MEET.
DID YOU EVER GET THE FEELING THAT YOU'RE IN LOVE--BUT YOU HAVE YET TO DISCOVER WHO WITH?
I AM TELLING YOU--THE BEST DONUTS IN SAN FRANCISCO.
SUDDENLY, I'M REMINDED OF EXACTLY WHERE I AM...
...EXACTLY NOWHERE.
KEEP THE CAMERA ON ME WHEN I'M TALKING.
YOU DON'T MIND IF I TRY THIS, DO YA?

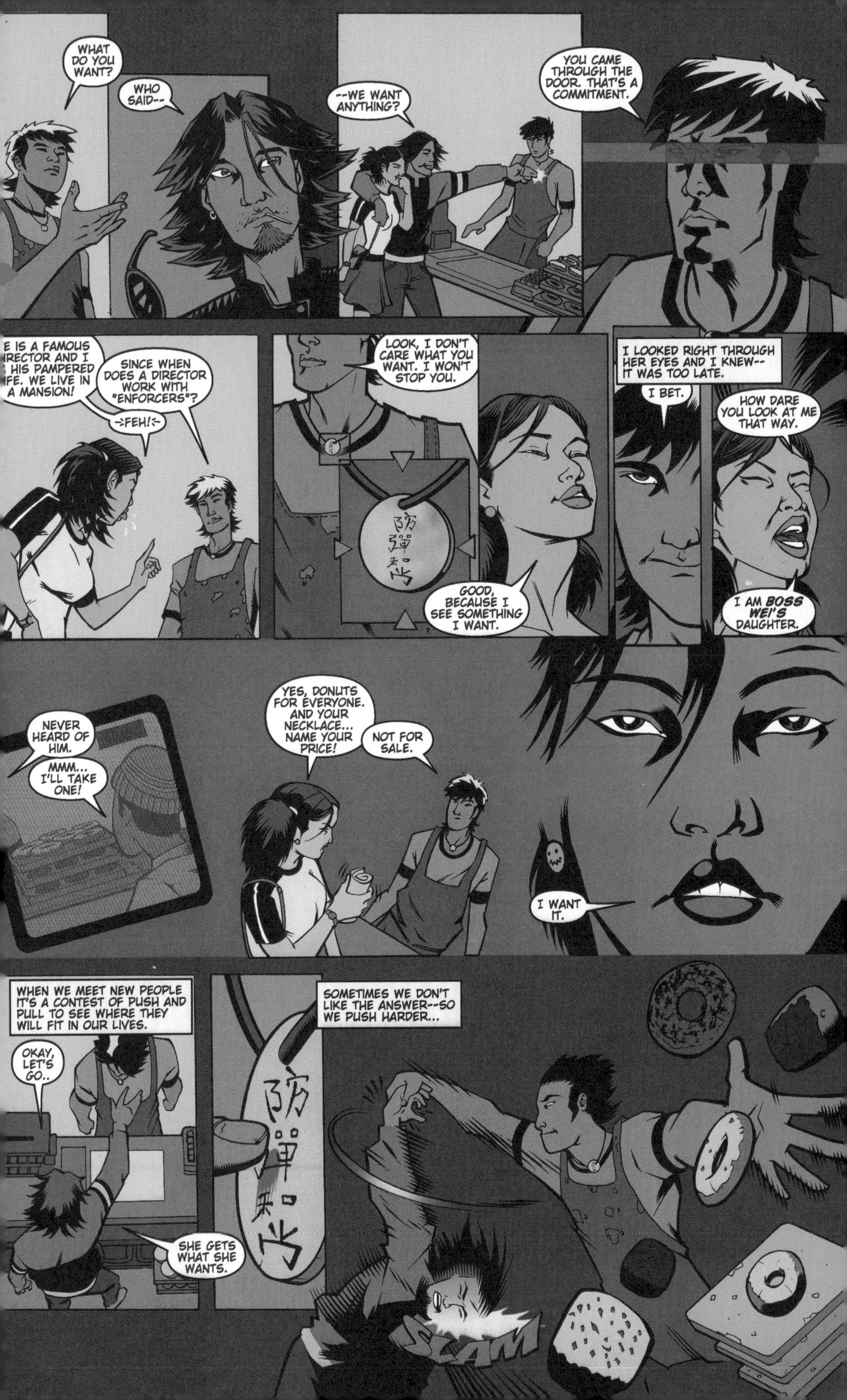
WHAT DO YOU WANT?
WHO SAID--
--WE WANT ANYTHING?
YOU CAME THROUGH THE DOOR. THAT'S A COMMITMENT.
E IS A FAMOUS IRECTOR AND I HIS PAMPERED IFE. WE LIVE IN A MANSION!
SINCE WHEN DOES A DIRECTOR WORK WITH "ENFORCERS"?
FEH!
LOOK, I DON'T CARE WHAT YOU WANT. I WON'T STOP YOU.
防弾和尚
GOOD, BECAUSE I SEE SOMETHING I WANT.
I LOOKED RIGHT THROUGH HER EYES AND I KNEW--IT WAS TOO LATE.
I BET.
HOW DARE YOU LOOK AT ME THAT WAY.
I AM BOSS WEI'S DAUGHTER.
NEVER HEARD OF HIM.
MMM... I'LL TAKE ONE!
YES, DONUTS FOR EVERYONE. AND YOUR NECKLACE... NAME YOUR PRICE!
NOT FOR SALE.
I WANT IT.
WHEN WE MEET NEW PEOPLE IT'S A CONTEST OF PUSH AND PULL TO SEE WHERE THEY WILL FIT IN OUR LIVES.
OKAY, LET'S GO..
SHE GETS WHAT SHE WANTS.
SOMETIMES WE DON'T LIKE THE ANSWER--SO WE PUSH HARDER...
SLAM

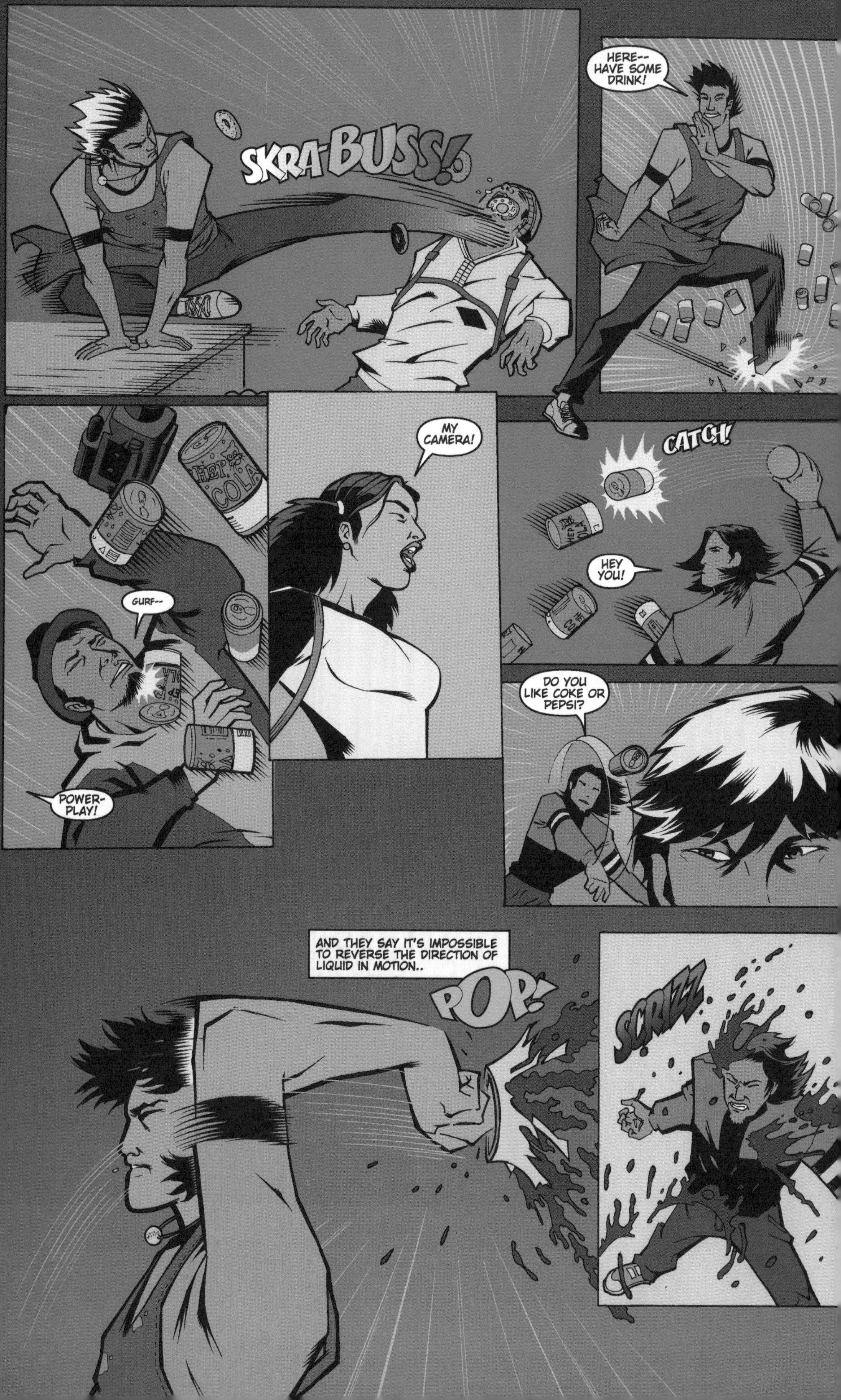

SKRA-BUSS!
HERE-- HAVE SOME DRINK!
GURF--
POWER-PLAY!
MY CAMERA!
CATCH!
HEY YOU!
DO YOU LIKE COKE OR PEPSI?
AND THEY SAY IT'S IMPOSSIBLE TO REVERSE THE DIRECTION OF LIQUID IN MOTION..
POP!
SCRIZZ

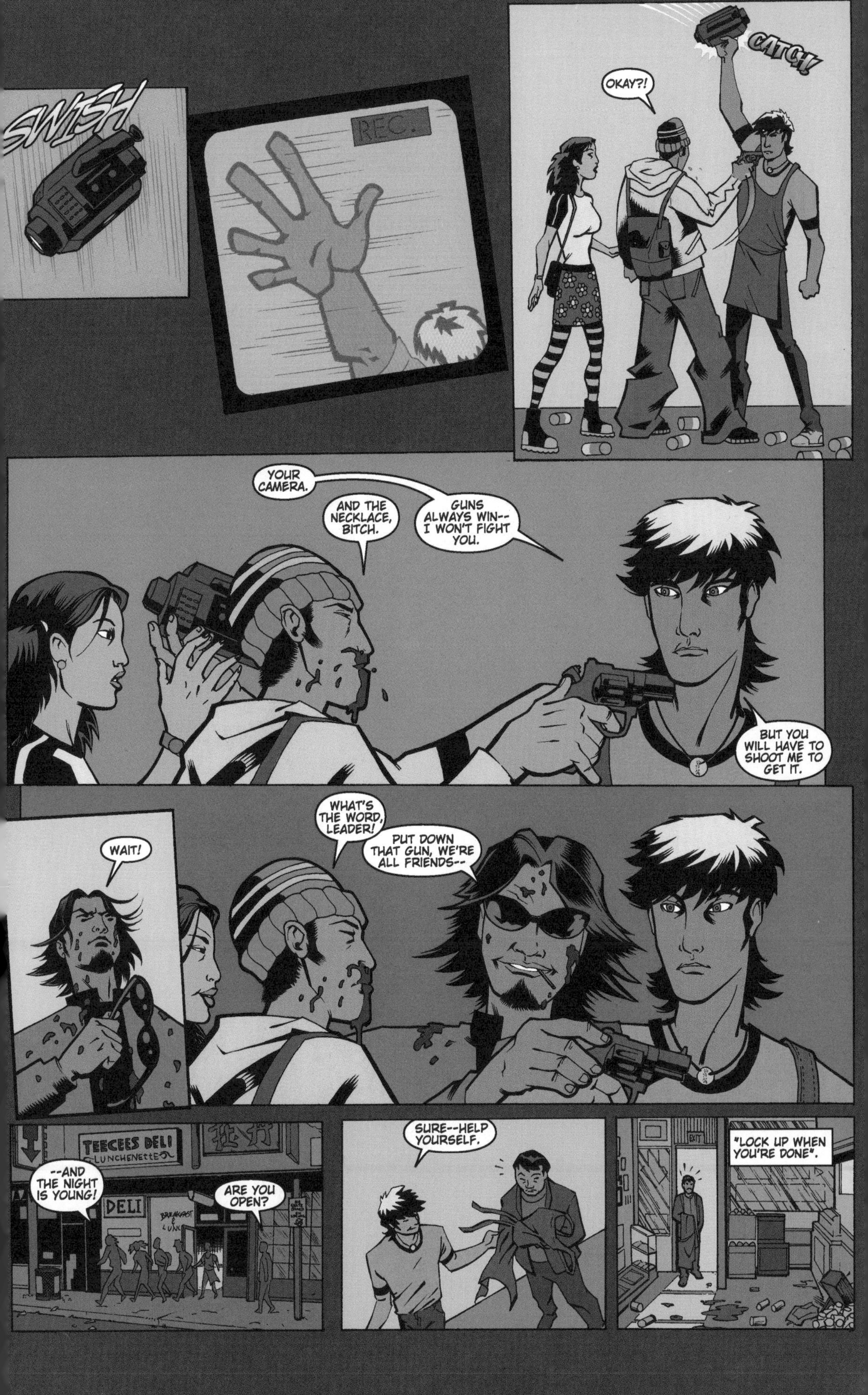
SWISH
REC.
OKAY?!
CATCH!
YOUR CAMERA.
AND THE NECKLACE, BITCH.
GUNS ALWAYS WIN-- I WON'T FIGHT YOU.
BUT YOU WILL HAVE TO SHOOT ME TO GET IT.
WAIT!
WHAT'S THE WORD, LEADER!
PUT DOWN THAT GUN, WE'RE ALL FRIENDS--
TEECEES DELI
LUNCHENETTE
DELI
--AND THE NIGHT IS YOUNG!
ARE YOU OPEN?
SURE--HELP YOURSELF.
"LOCK UP WHEN YOU'RE DONE".

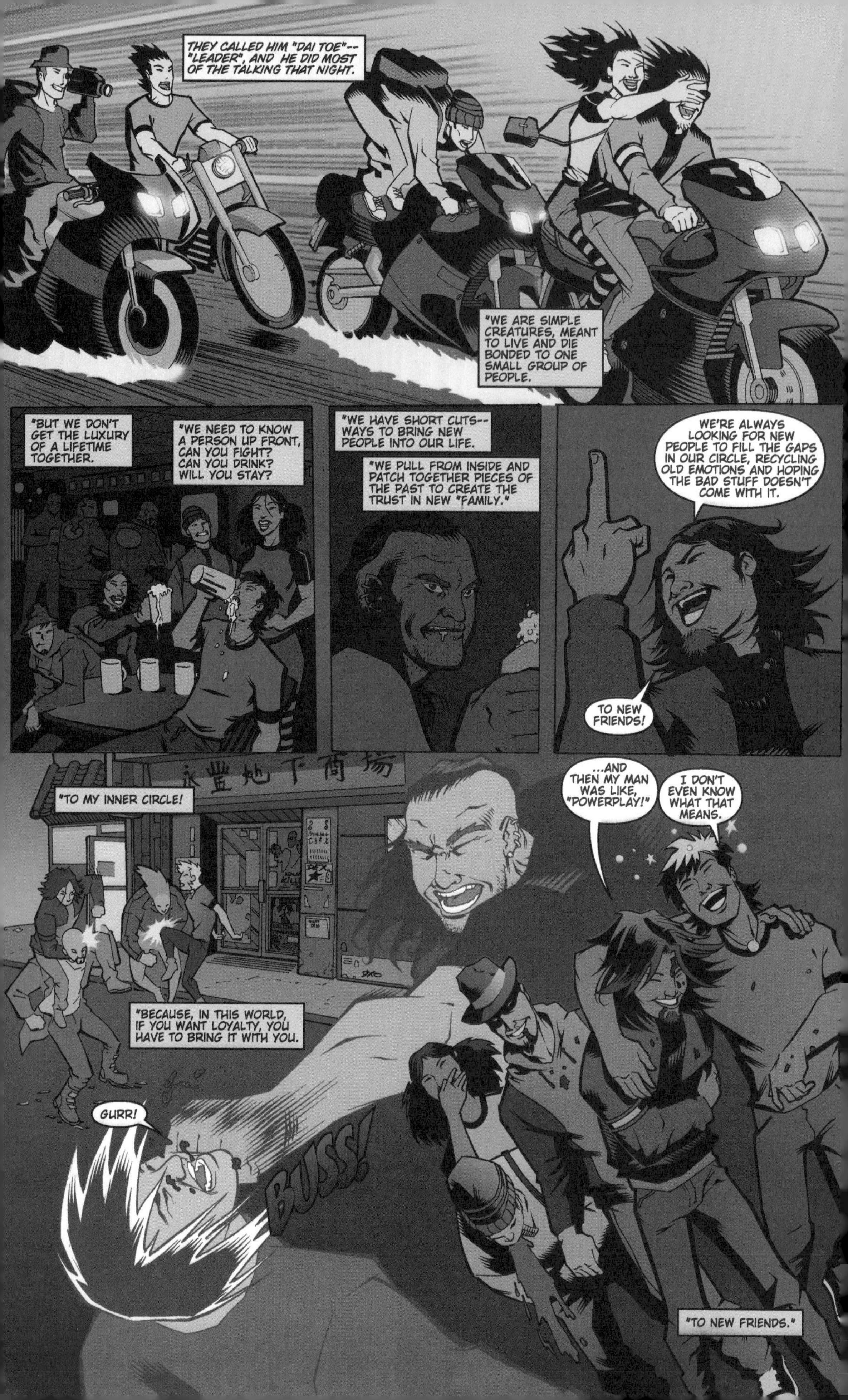
THEY CALLED HIM "DAI TOE"-- "LEADER", AND HE DID MOST OF THE TALKING THAT NIGHT.
"WE ARE SIMPLE CREATURES, MEANT TO LIVE AND DIE BONDED TO ONE SMALL GROUP OF PEOPLE.
"BUT WE DON'T GET THE LUXURY OF A LIFETIME TOGETHER.
"WE NEED TO KNOW A PERSON UP FRONT, CAN YOU FIGHT? CAN YOU DRINK? WILL YOU STAY?
"WE HAVE SHORT CUTS-- WAYS TO BRING NEW PEOPLE INTO OUR LIFE.
"WE PULL FROM INSIDE AND PATCH TOGETHER PIECES OF THE PAST TO CREATE THE TRUST IN NEW "FAMILY."
WE'RE ALWAYS LOOKING FOR NEW PEOPLE TO FILL THE GAPS IN OUR CIRCLE, RECYCLING OLD EMOTIONS AND HOPING THE BAD STUFF DOESN'T COME WITH IT.
TO NEW FRIENDS!
永豊地下商場
"TO MY INNER CIRCLE!
...AND THEN MY MAN WAS LIKE, "POWERPLAY!"
I DON'T EVEN KNOW WHAT THAT MEANS.
"BECAUSE, IN THIS WORLD, IF YOU WANT LOYALTY, YOU HAVE TO BRING IT WITH YOU.
GURR!
BUSS!
"TO NEW FRIENDS."

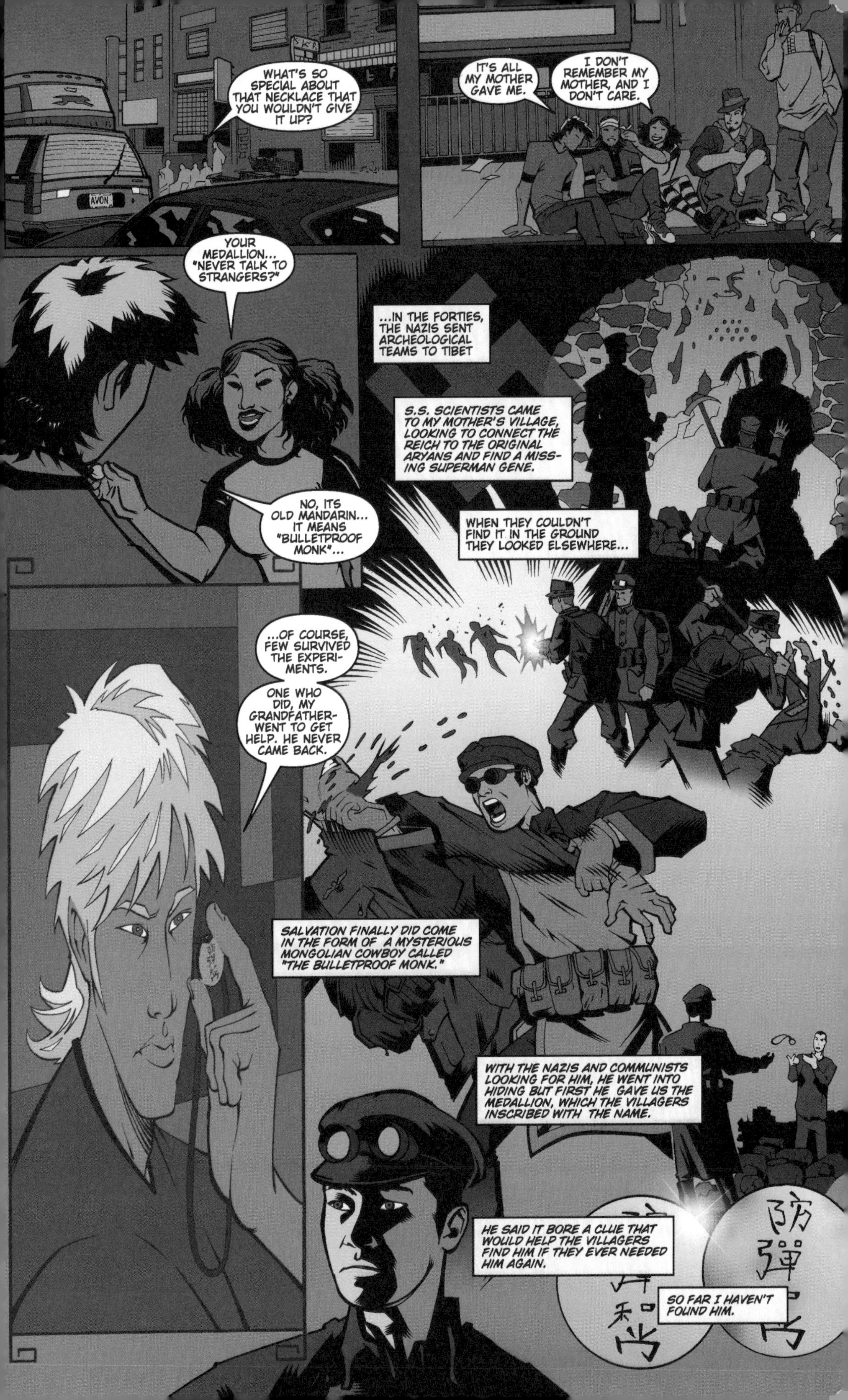
WHAT'S SO SPECIAL ABOUT THAT NECKLACE THAT YOU WOULDN'T GIVE IT UP?
AVON
IT'S ALL MY MOTHER GAVE ME.
I DON'T REMEMBER MY MOTHER, AND I DON'T CARE.
YOUR MEDALLION... "NEVER TALK TO STRANGERS?"
NO, ITS OLD MANDARIN... IT MEANS "BULLETPROOF MONK"...
...IN THE FORTIES, THE NAZIS SENT ARCHEOLOGICAL TEAMS TO TIBET
S.S. SCIENTISTS CAME TO MY MOTHER'S VILLAGE, LOOKING TO CONNECT THE REICH TO THE ORIGINAL ARYANS AND FIND A MISSING SUPERMAN GENE.
WHEN THEY COULDN'T FIND IT IN THE GROUND THEY LOOKED ELSEWHERE...
...OF COURSE, FEW SURVIVED THE EXPERIMENTS.
ONE WHO DID, MY GRANDFATHER- WENT TO GET HELP. HE NEVER CAME BACK.
SALVATION FINALLY DID COME IN THE FORM OF A MYSTERIOUS MONGOLIAN COWBOY CALLED "THE BULLETPROOF MONK."
WITH THE NAZIS AND COMMUNISTS LOOKING FOR HIM, HE WENT INTO HIDING BUT FIRST HE GAVE US THE MEDALLION, WHICH THE VILLAGERS INSCRIBED WITH THE NAME.
HE SAID IT BORE A CLUE THAT WOULD HELP THE VILLAGERS FIND HIM IF THEY EVER NEEDED HIM AGAIN.
SO FAR I HAVEN'T FOUND HIM.

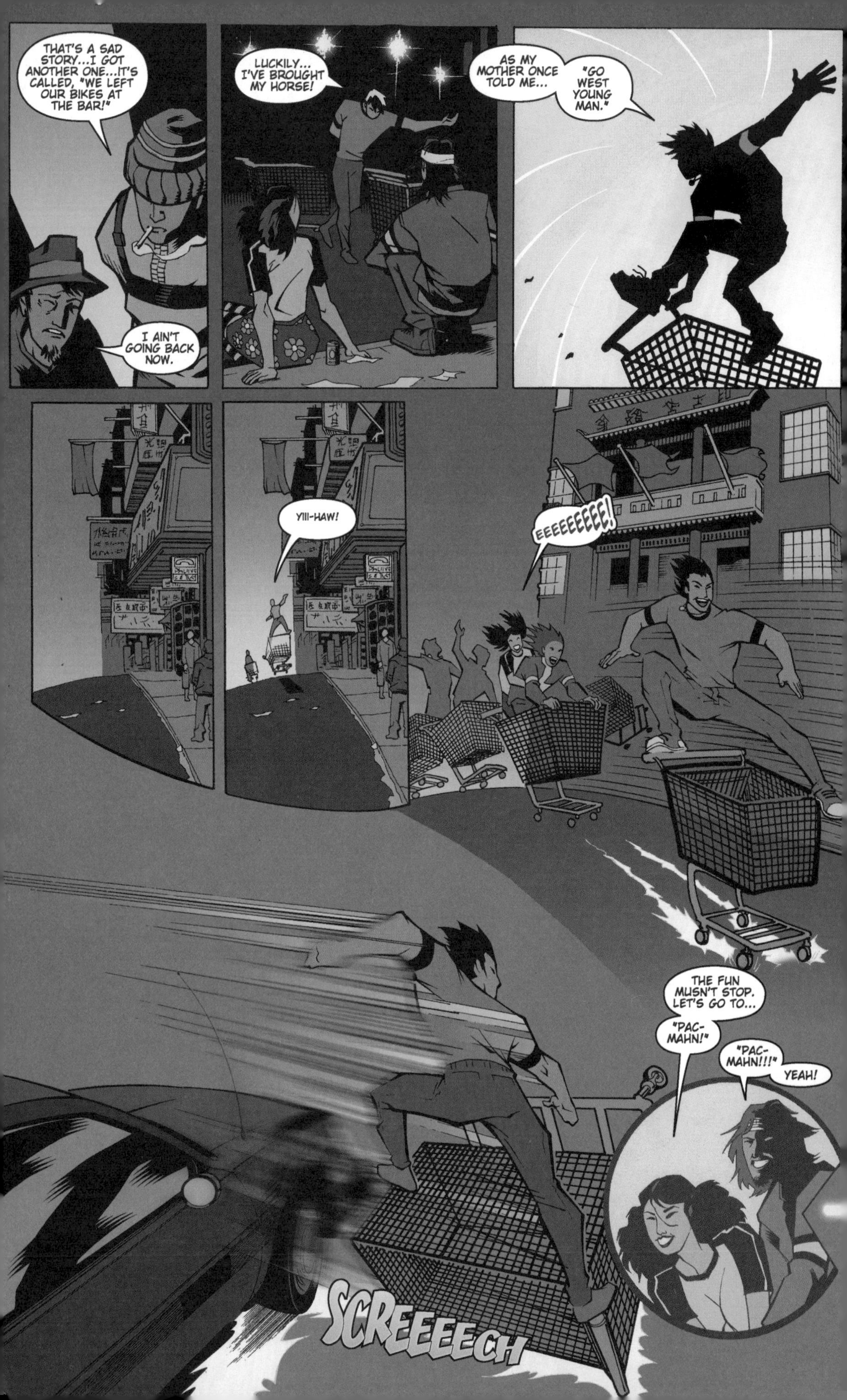
THAT'S A SAD STORY...I GOT ANOTHER ONE...IT'S CALLED, "WE LEFT OUR BIKES AT THE BAR!"
I AIN'T GOING BACK NOW.
LUCKILY... I'VE BROUGHT MY HORSE!
AS MY MOTHER ONCE TOLD ME...
"GO WEST YOUNG MAN."
YIII-HAW!
EEEEEEEEE!
THE FUN MUSN'T STOP. LET'S GO TO...
"PAC-MAHN!"
"PAC-MAHN!!!"
YEAH!
SCREEEEECH

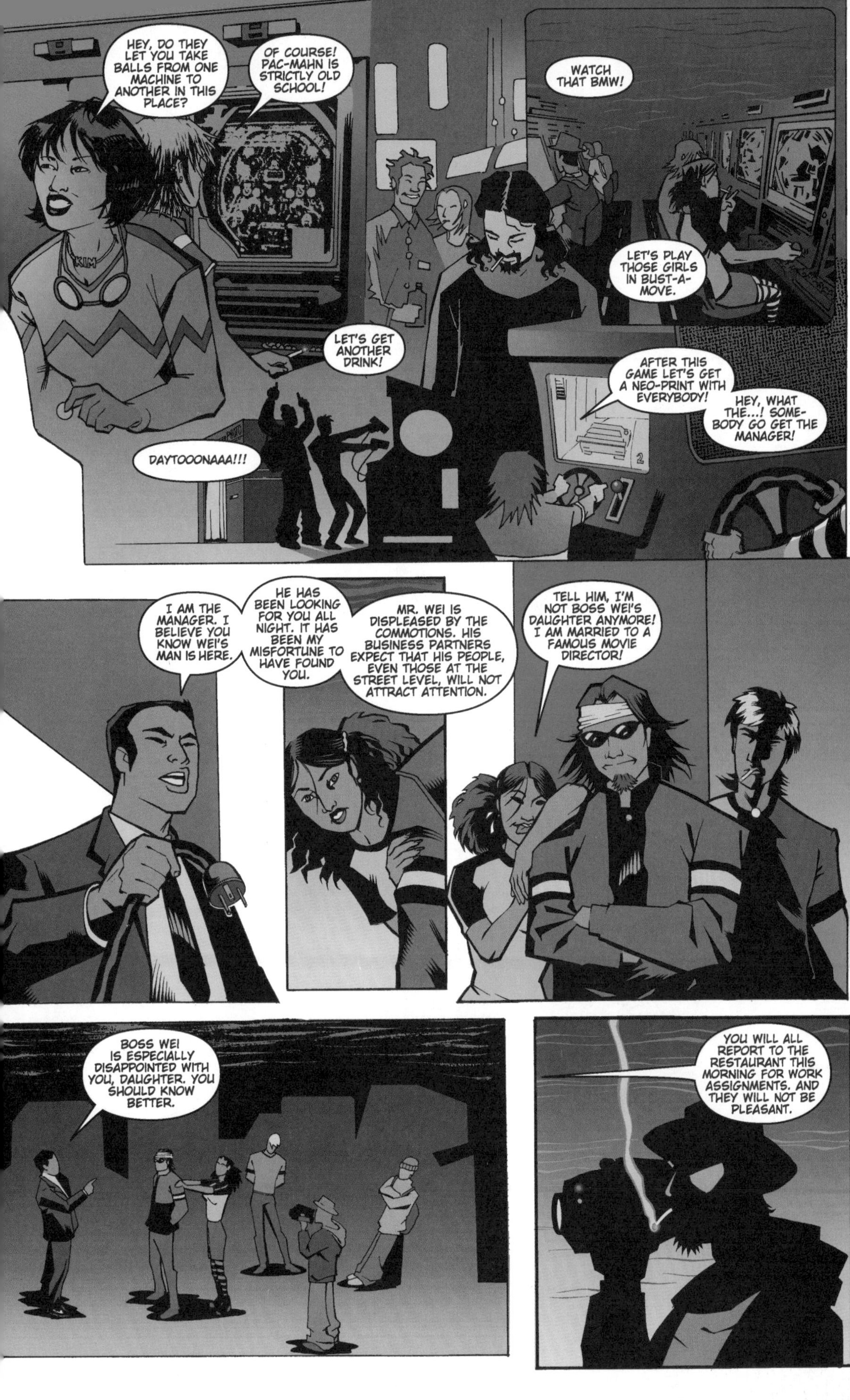
HEY, DO THEY LET YOU TAKE BALLS FROM ONE MACHINE TO ANOTHER IN THIS PLACE?
OF COURSE! PAC-MAHN IS STRICTLY OLD SCHOOL!
WATCH THAT BMW!
LET'S PLAY THOSE GIRLS IN BUST-A-MOVE.
LET'S GET ANOTHER DRINK!
AFTER THIS GAME LET'S GET A NEO-PRINT WITH EVERYBODY!
HEY, WHAT THE...! SOMEBODY GO GET THE MANAGER!
DAYTOOONAAA!!!
I AM THE MANAGER. I BELIEVE YOU KNOW WEI'S MAN IS HERE.
HE HAS BEEN LOOKING FOR YOU ALL NIGHT. IT HAS BEEN MY MISFORTUNE TO HAVE FOUND YOU.
MR. WEI IS DISPLEASED BY THE COMMOTIONS. HIS BUSINESS PARTNERS EXPECT THAT HIS PEOPLE, EVEN THOSE AT THE STREET LEVEL, WILL NOT ATTRACT ATTENTION.
TELL HIM, I'M NOT BOSS WEI'S DAUGHTER ANYMORE! I AM MARRIED TO A FAMOUS MOVIE DIRECTOR!
BOSS WEI IS ESPECIALLY DISAPPOINTED WITH YOU, DAUGHTER. YOU SHOULD KNOW BETTER.
YOU WILL ALL REPORT TO THE RESTAURANT THIS MORNING FOR WORK ASSIGNMENTS. AND THEY WILL NOT BE PLEASANT.

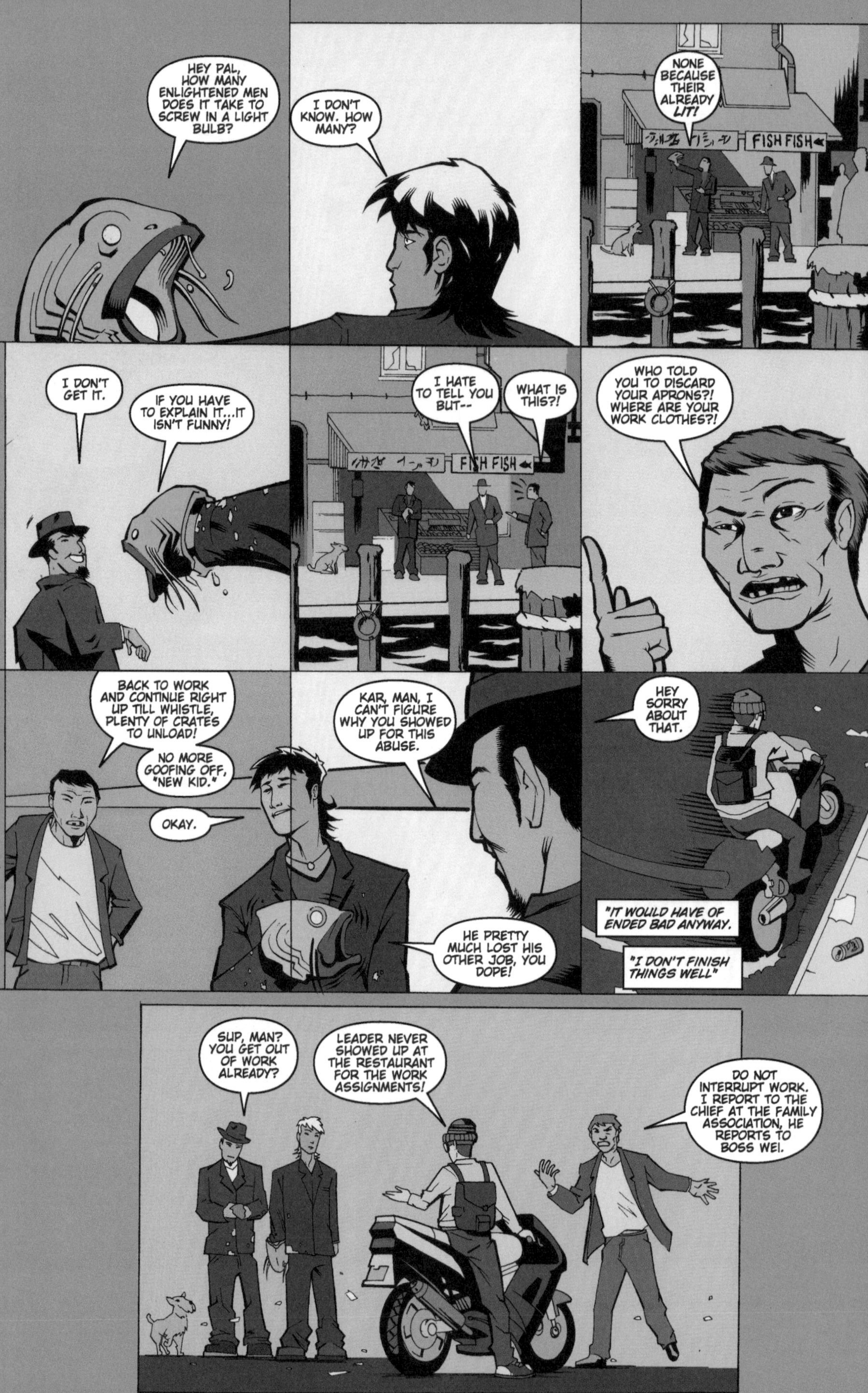
HEY PAL, HOW MANY ENLIGHTENED MEN DOES IT TAKE TO SCREW IN A LIGHT BULB?
I DON'T KNOW. HOW MANY?
NONE BECAUSE THEIR ALREADY LIT!
FISH FISH
I DON'T GET IT.
IF YOU HAVE TO EXPLAIN IT...IT ISN'T FUNNY!
I HATE TO TELL YOU BUT--
WHAT IS THIS?!
FISH FISH
WHO TOLD YOU TO DISCARD YOUR APRONS?! WHERE ARE YOUR WORK CLOTHES?!
BACK TO WORK AND CONTINUE RIGHT UP TILL WHISTLE, PLENTY OF CRATES TO UNLOAD!
NO MORE GOOFING OFF, "NEW KID."
OKAY.
KAR, MAN, I CAN'T FIGURE WHY YOU SHOWED UP FOR THIS ABUSE.
HE PRETTY MUCH LOST HIS OTHER JOB, YOU DOPE!
HEY SORRY ABOUT THAT.
"IT WOULD HAVE OF ENDED BAD ANYWAY.
"I DON'T FINISH THINGS WELL"
SUP, MAN? YOU GET OUT OF WORK ALREADY?
LEADER NEVER SHOWED UP AT THE RESTAURANT FOR THE WORK ASSIGNMENTS!
DO NOT INTERRUPT WORK. I REPORT TO THE CHIEF AT THE FAMILY ASSOCIATION, HE REPORTS TO BOSS WEI.

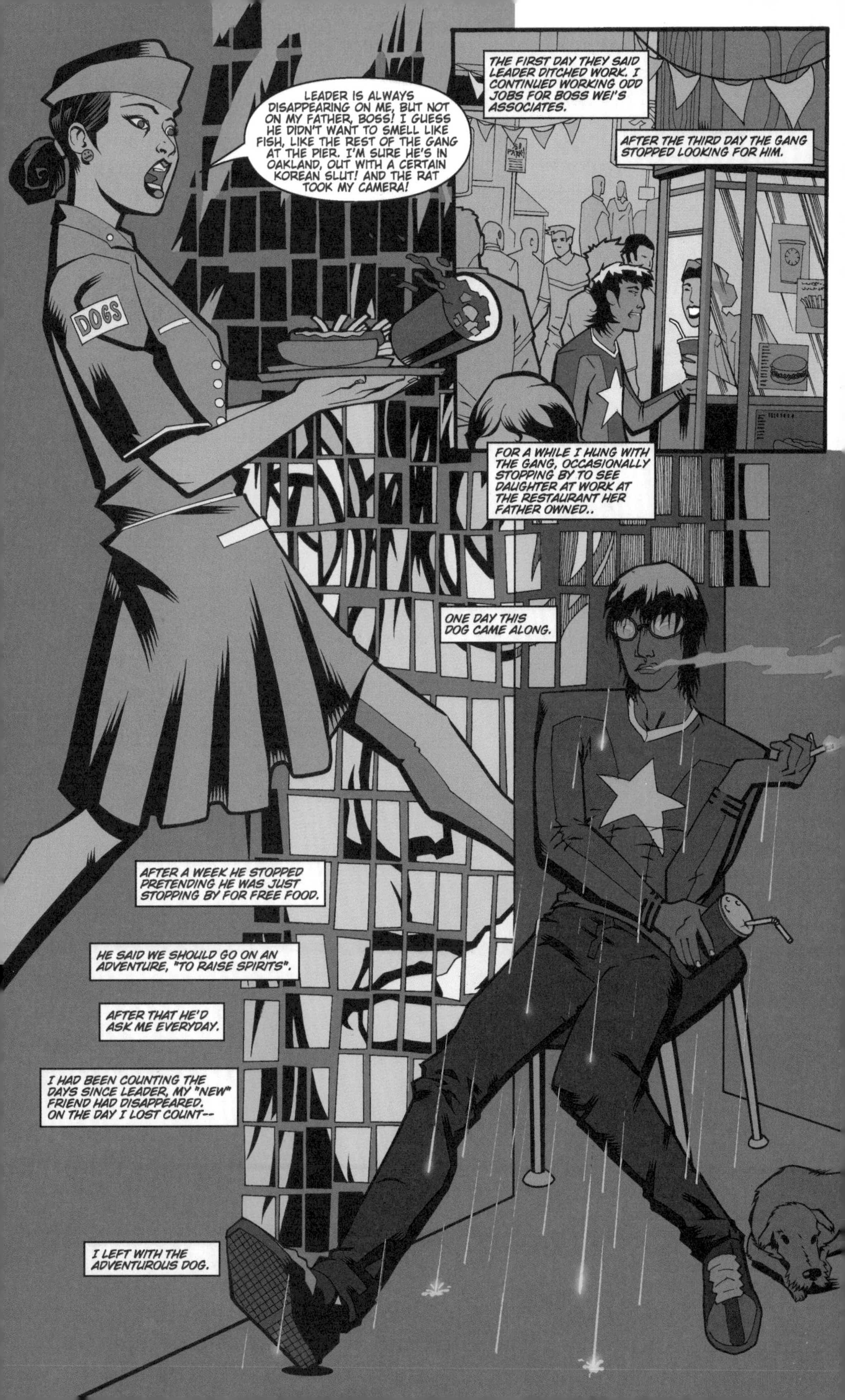
THE FIRST DAY THEY SAID LEADER DITCHED WORK. I CONTINUED WORKING ODD JOBS FOR BOSS WEI'S ASSOCIATES.
AFTER THE THIRD DAY THE GANG STOPPED LOOKING FOR HIM.
LEADER IS ALWAYS DISAPPEARING ON ME, BUT NOT ON MY FATHER, BOSS! I GUESS HE DIDN'T WANT TO SMELL LIKE FISH, LIKE THE REST OF THE GANG AT THE PIER. I'M SURE HE'S IN OAKLAND, OUT WITH A CERTAIN KOREAN SLUT! AND THE RAT TOOK MY CAMERA!
DOGS
FOR A WHILE I HUNG WITH THE GANG, OCCASIONALLY STOPPING BY TO SEE DAUGHTER AT WORK AT THE RESTAURANT HER FATHER OWNED..
ONE DAY THIS DOG CAME ALONG.
AFTER A WEEK HE STOPPED PRETENDING HE WAS JUST STOPPING BY FOR FREE FOOD.
HE SAID WE SHOULD GO ON AN ADVENTURE, "TO RAISE SPIRITS".
AFTER THAT HE'D ASK ME EVERYDAY.
I HAD BEEN COUNTING THE DAYS SINCE LEADER, MY "NEW" FRIEND HAD DISAPPEARED. ON THE DAY I LOST COUNT--
I LEFT WITH THE ADVENTUROUS DOG.

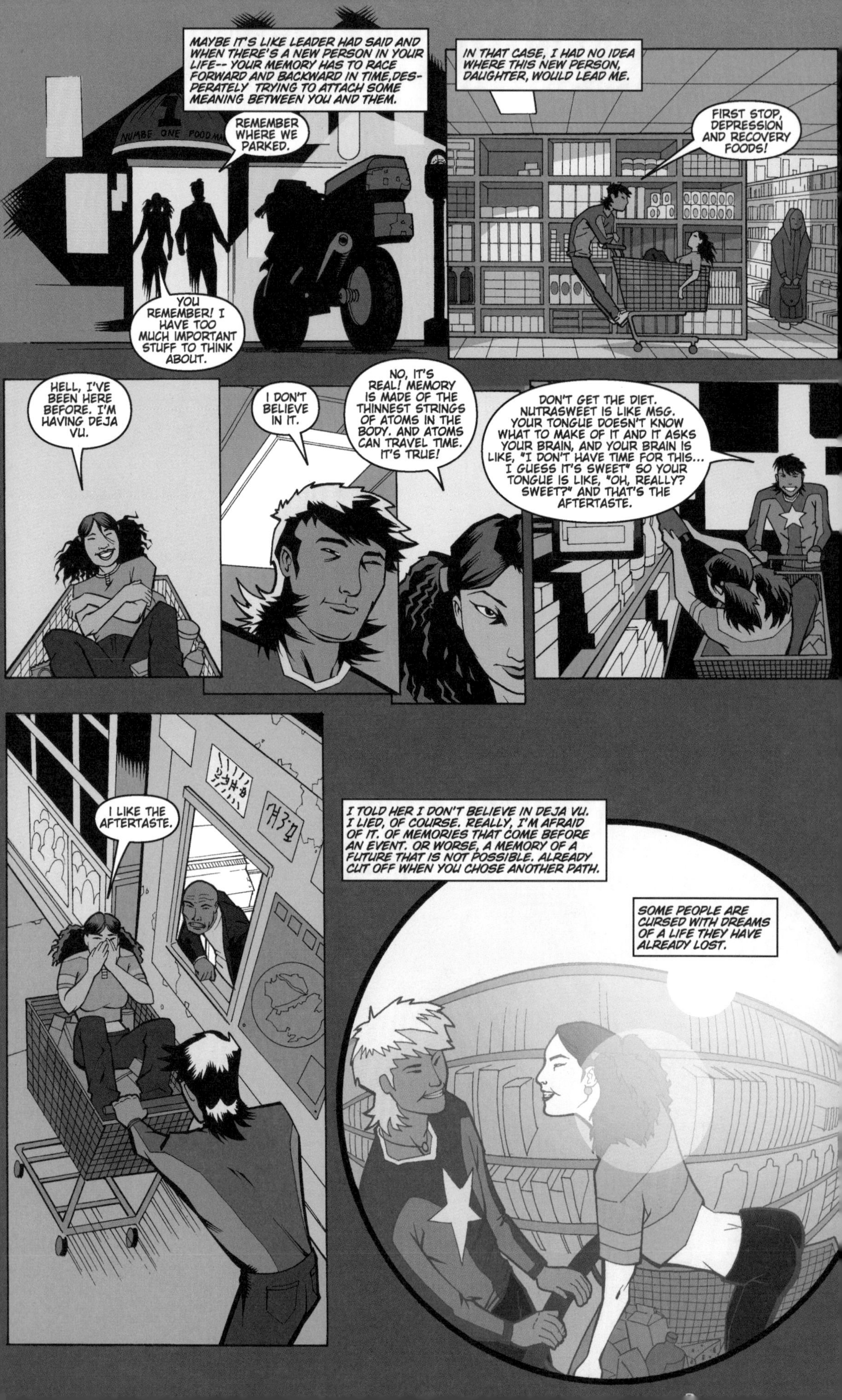
MAYBE IT'S LIKE LEADER HAD SAID AND WHEN THERE'S A NEW PERSON IN YOUR LIFE-- YOUR MEMORY HAS TO RACE FORWARD AND BACKWARD IN TIME, DESPERATELY TRYING TO ATTACH SOME MEANING BETWEEN YOU AND THEM.
NUMBE ONE FOOD MA
REMEMBER WHERE WE PARKED.
YOU REMEMBER! I HAVE TOO MUCH IMPORTANT STUFF TO THINK ABOUT.
IN THAT CASE, I HAD NO IDEA WHERE THIS NEW PERSON, DAUGHTER, WOULD LEAD ME.
FIRST STOP, DEPRESSION AND RECOVERY FOODS!
HELL, I'VE BEEN HERE BEFORE. I'M HAVING DEJA VU.
I DON'T BELIEVE IN IT.
NO, IT'S REAL! MEMORY IS MADE OF THE THINNEST STRINGS OF ATOMS IN THE BODY. AND ATOMS CAN TRAVEL TIME. IT'S TRUE!
DON'T GET THE DIET. NUTRASWEET IS LIKE MSG. YOUR TONGUE DOESN'T KNOW WHAT TO MAKE OF IT AND IT ASKS YOUR BRAIN, AND YOUR BRAIN IS LIKE, "I DON'T HAVE TIME FOR THIS... I GUESS IT'S SWEET" SO YOUR TONGUE IS LIKE, "OH, REALLY? SWEET?" AND THAT'S THE AFTERTASTE.
I LIKE THE AFTERTASTE.
I TOLD HER I DON'T BELIEVE IN DEJA VU. I LIED, OF COURSE. REALLY, I'M AFRAID OF IT. OF MEMORIES THAT COME BEFORE AN EVENT. OR WORSE, A MEMORY OF A FUTURE THAT IS NOT POSSIBLE. ALREADY CUT OFF WHEN YOU CHOSE ANOTHER PATH.
SOME PEOPLE ARE CURSED WITH DREAMS OF A LIFE THEY HAVE ALREADY LOST.

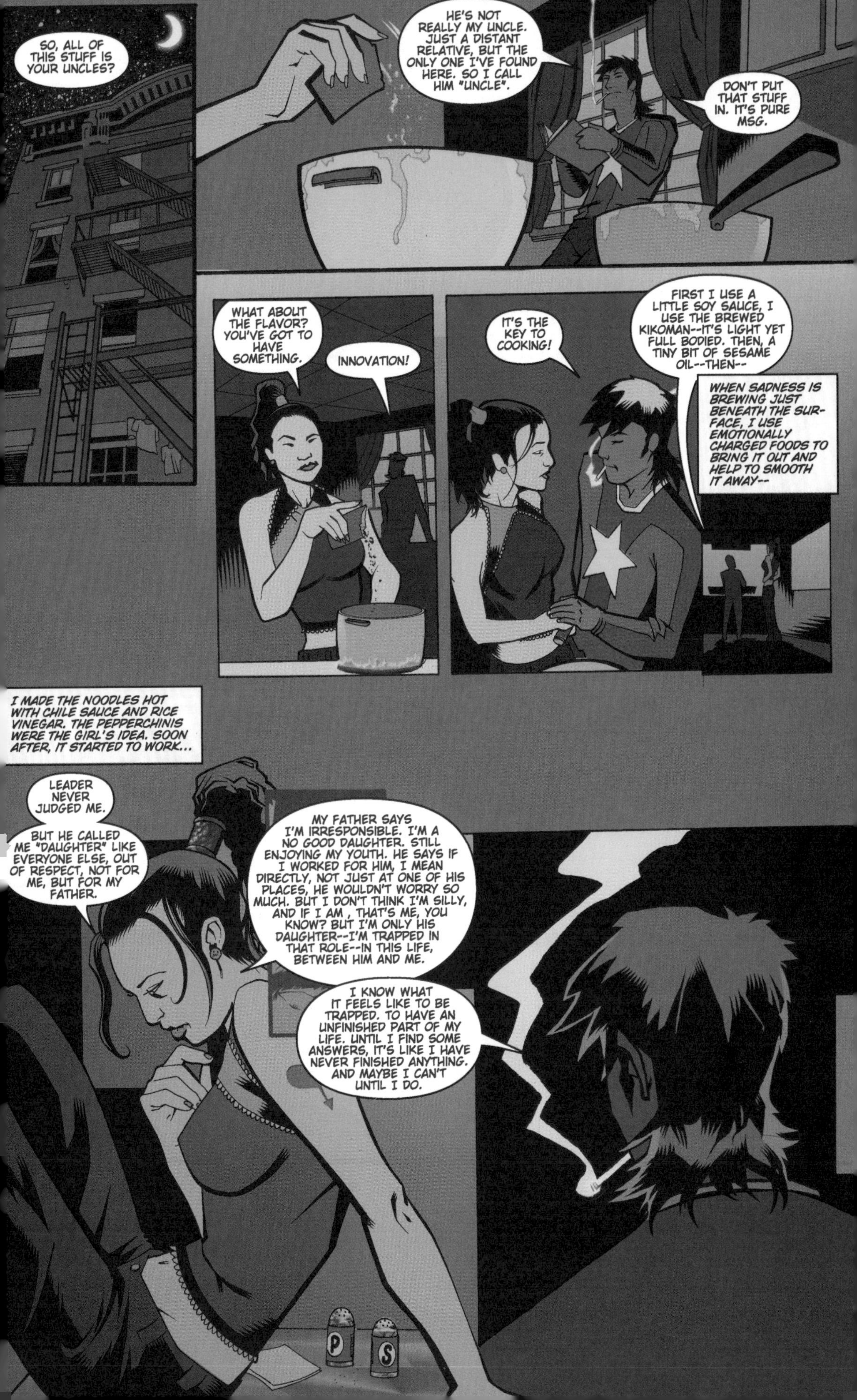
SO, ALL OF THIS STUFF IS YOUR UNCLES?
HE'S NOT REALLY MY UNCLE. JUST A DISTANT RELATIVE, BUT THE ONLY ONE I'VE FOUND HERE. SO I CALL HIM "UNCLE".
DON'T PUT THAT STUFF IN. IT'S PURE MSG.
WHAT ABOUT THE FLAVOR? YOU'VE GOT TO HAVE SOMETHING.
INNOVATION!
IT'S THE KEY TO COOKING!
FIRST I USE A LITTLE SOY SAUCE, I USE THE BREWED KIKOMAN--IT'S LIGHT YET FULL BODIED. THEN, A TINY BIT OF SESAME OIL--THEN--
WHEN SADNESS IS BREWING JUST BENEATH THE SURFACE, I USE EMOTIONALLY CHARGED FOODS TO BRING IT OUT AND HELP TO SMOOTH IT AWAY--
I MADE THE NOODLES HOT WITH CHILE SAUCE AND RICE VINEGAR. THE PEPPERCHINIS WERE THE GIRL'S IDEA. SOON AFTER, IT STARTED TO WORK...
LEADER NEVER JUDGED ME.
BUT HE CALLED ME "DAUGHTER" LIKE EVERYONE ELSE, OUT OF RESPECT, NOT FOR ME, BUT FOR MY FATHER.
MY FATHER SAYS I'M IRRESPONSIBLE. I'M A NO GOOD DAUGHTER. STILL ENJOYING MY YOUTH. HE SAYS IF I WORKED FOR HIM, I MEAN DIRECTLY, NOT JUST AT ONE OF HIS PLACES, HE WOULDN'T WORRY SO MUCH. BUT I DON'T THINK I'M SILLY, AND IF I AM , THAT'S ME, YOU KNOW? BUT I'M ONLY HIS DAUGHTER--I'M TRAPPED IN THAT ROLE--IN THIS LIFE, BETWEEN HIM AND ME.
I KNOW WHAT IT FEELS LIKE TO BE TRAPPED. TO HAVE AN UNFINISHED PART OF MY LIFE. UNTIL I FIND SOME ANSWERS, IT'S LIKE I HAVE NEVER FINISHED ANYTHING. AND MAYBE I CAN'T UNTIL I DO.
P
S

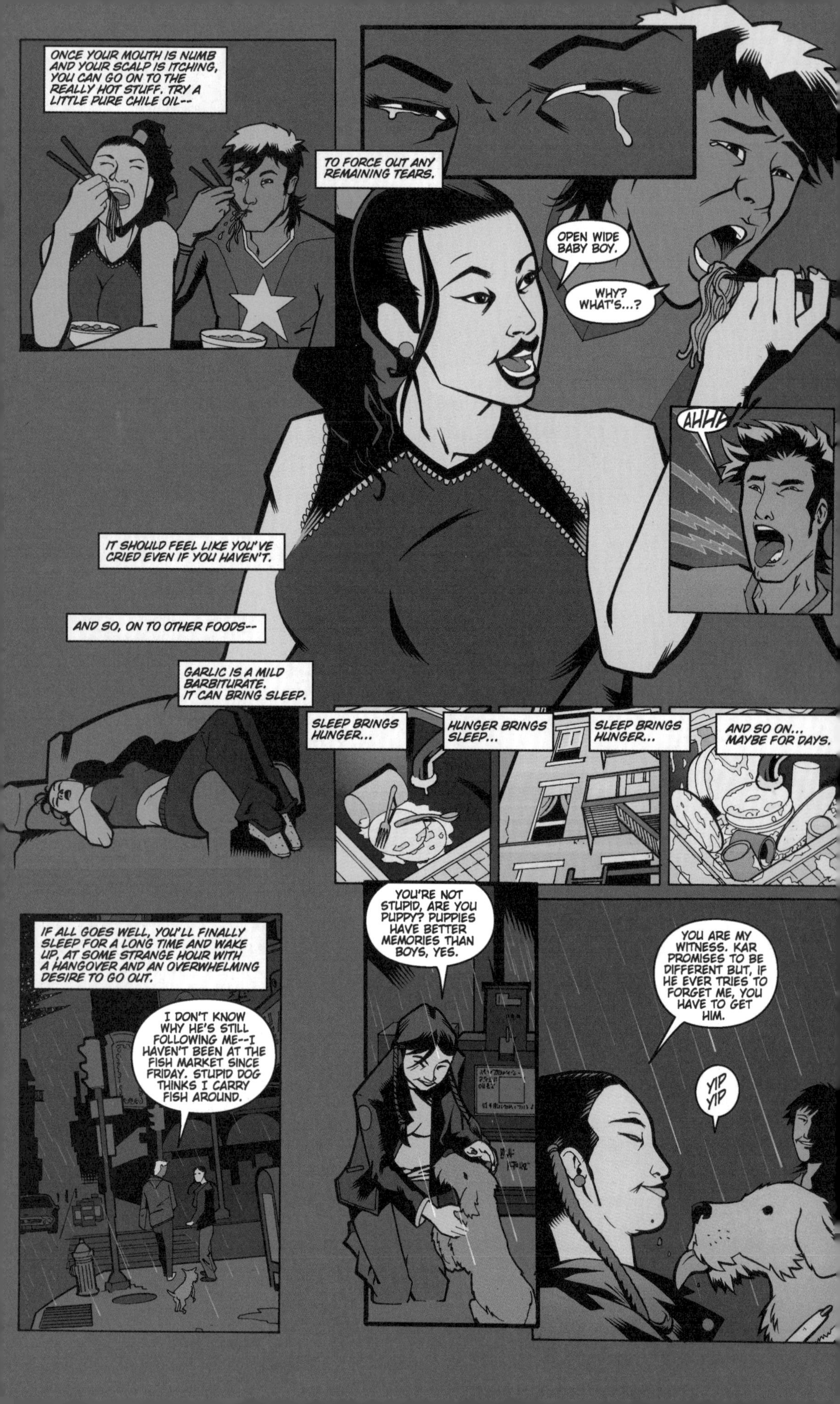
ONCE YOUR MOUTH IS NUMB AND YOUR SCALP IS ITCHING, YOU CAN GO ON TO THE REALLY HOT STUFF. TRY A LITTLE PURE CHILE OIL--
TO FORCE OUT ANY REMAINING TEARS.
OPEN WIDE BABY BOY.
WHY? WHAT'S...?
AHHH
IT SHOULD FEEL LIKE YOU'VE CRIED EVEN IF YOU HAVEN'T.
AND SO, ON TO OTHER FOODS--
GARLIC IS A MILD BARBITURATE. IT CAN BRING SLEEP.
SLEEP BRINGS HUNGER...
HUNGER BRINGS SLEEP...
SLEEP BRINGS HUNGER...
AND SO ON... MAYBE FOR DAYS.
IF ALL GOES WELL, YOU'LL FINALLY SLEEP FOR A LONG TIME AND WAKE UP, AT SOME STRANGE HOUR WITH A HANGOVER AND AN OVERWHELMING DESIRE TO GO OUT.
I DON'T KNOW WHY HE'S STILL FOLLOWING ME--I HAVEN'T BEEN AT THE FISH MARKET SINCE FRIDAY. STUPID DOG THINKS I CARRY FISH AROUND.
YOU'RE NOT STUPID, ARE YOU PUPPY? PUPPIES HAVE BETTER MEMORIES THAN BOYS, YES.
YOU ARE MY WITNESS. KAR PROMISES TO BE DIFFERENT BUT, IF HE EVER TRIES TO FORGET ME, YOU HAVE TO GET HIM.
YIP YIP

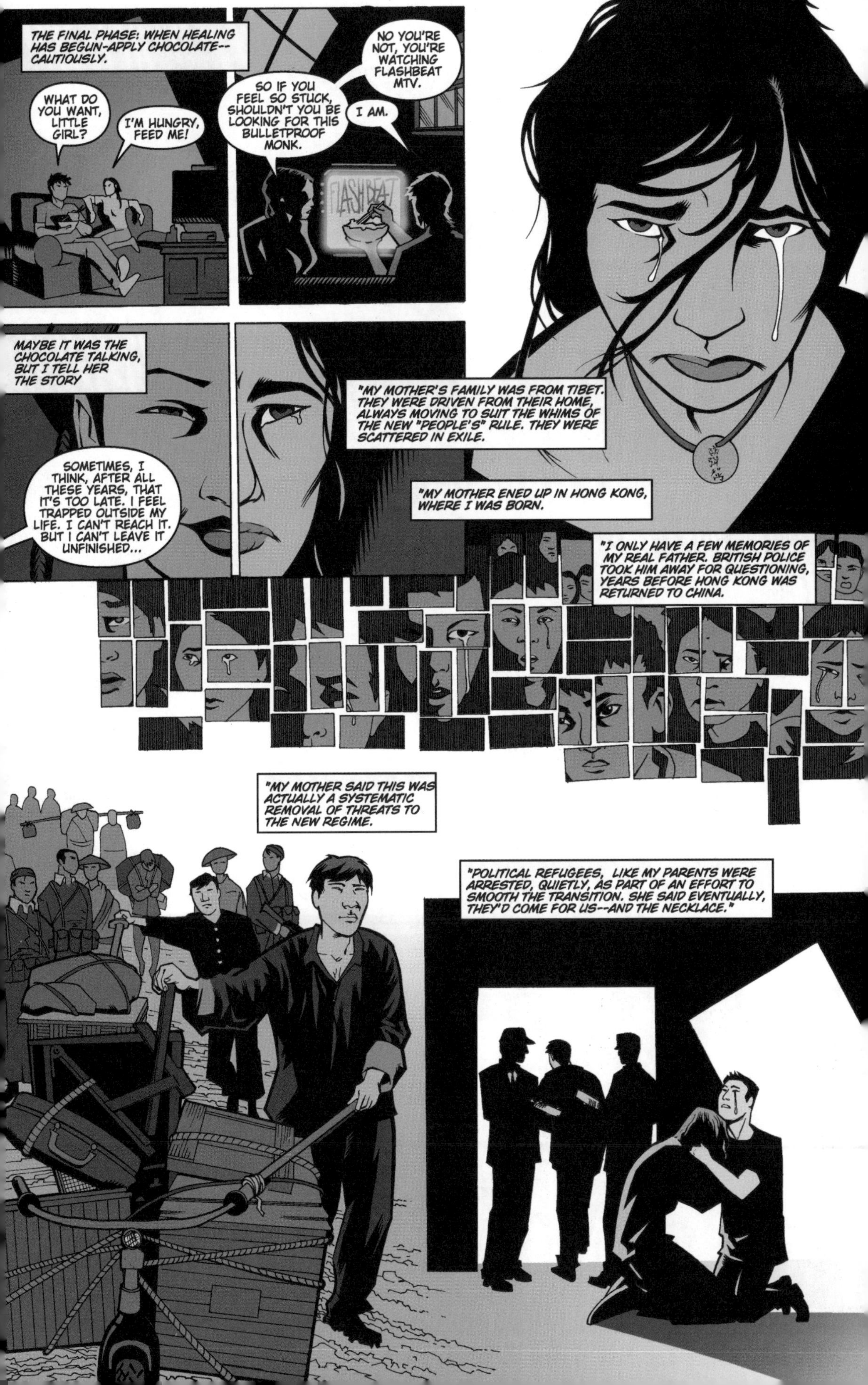
THE FINAL PHASE: WHEN HEALING HAS BEGUN-APPLY CHOCOLATE--CAUTIOUSLY.
WHAT DO YOU WANT, LITTLE GIRL?
I'M HUNGRY, FEED ME!
SO IF YOU FEEL SO STUCK, SHOULDN'T YOU BE LOOKING FOR THIS BULLETPROOF MONK.
I AM.
NO YOU'RE NOT, YOU'RE WATCHING FLASHBEAT MTV.
FLASHBEAT
MAYBE IT WAS THE CHOCOLATE TALKING, BUT I TELL HER THE STORY
SOMETIMES, I THINK, AFTER ALL THESE YEARS, THAT IT'S TOO LATE. I FEEL TRAPPED OUTSIDE MY LIFE. I CAN'T REACH IT. BUT I CAN'T LEAVE IT UNFINISHED...
"MY MOTHER'S FAMILY WAS FROM TIBET. THEY WERE DRIVEN FROM THEIR HOME, ALWAYS MOVING TO SUIT THE WHIMS OF THE NEW "PEOPLE'S" RULE. THEY WERE SCATTERED IN EXILE.
"MY MOTHER ENED UP IN HONG KONG, WHERE I WAS BORN.
"I ONLY HAVE A FEW MEMORIES OF MY REAL FATHER. BRITISH POLICE TOOK HIM AWAY FOR QUESTIONING, YEARS BEFORE HONG KONG WAS RETURNED TO CHINA.
"MY MOTHER SAID THIS WAS ACTUALLY A SYSTEMATIC REMOVAL OF THREATS TO THE NEW REGIME.
"POLITICAL REFUGEES, LIKE MY PARENTS WERE ARRESTED, QUIETLY, AS PART OF AN EFFORT TO SMOOTH THE TRANSITION. SHE SAID EVENTUALLY, THEY'D COME FOR US--AND THE NECKLACE."

"I DIDN'T WANT TO LEAVE. I WAS SEVEN YEARS OLD-- ALL MY FRIENDS AND PEOPLE I KNEW AS FAMILY."

"SHE SAID IF I LOOKED FOR THE MONK I'D BE SAFE. AND OUR FAMILY WOULD BE FREE."

"I KNEW I'D NEVER SEE HER AGAIN! SHE SAID "THE HEART KNOWS NO TIME"... AN OLD SAYING THAT SHE SAID MEANT SHE'D ALWAYS BE WITH ME."

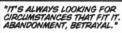

"I BLAMED HER. EVEN NOW THAT I KNOW HER REASONS...PART OF ME CAN'T FORGIVE HER FOR LEAVING...SHE SAID PEOPLE WOULD TRY TO GET THE NECKLACE. SHE SENT ME TO A COUSIN IN TAIWAN."

"I'M UNSURE WHERE TO LOOK NEXT. WHERE TO EVEN START, BUT I CAN'T DO ANYTHING ELSE, EITHER.

"MAYBE THE HEART KNOWS NO TIME, BUT THERE IS A BAD SIDE TO THAT, AT ITS CORE, MY HEART STILL FEELS THE WAY IT DID THAT DAY. IT IS FROZEN IN THE PAST. THE HEART WILL CARRY AN UNFINISHED FEELING FOR A LIFETIME, LOOKING FOR A NEW PLACE FOR THEM TO GROW."

"IT'S ALWAYS LOOKING FOR CIRCUMSTANCES THAT FIT IT. ABANDONMENT, BETRAYAL."

I'VE BEEN MOVING EVER SINCE.

YOU CAN'T KEEP RUNNING FOREVER.

THAT'S WHAT MY UNCLE ALWAYS SAYS.

LOOK AT YOU--YOU ARE COVERED IN ICE CREAM.

YOU ARE SILLY.

I DON'T WANT TO BE SILLY.

YOU RISK YOUR SECRETS WHEN YOU EAT WITH SOME- ONE ELSE. BUT AFTERWARDS, THERE IS A BOND.

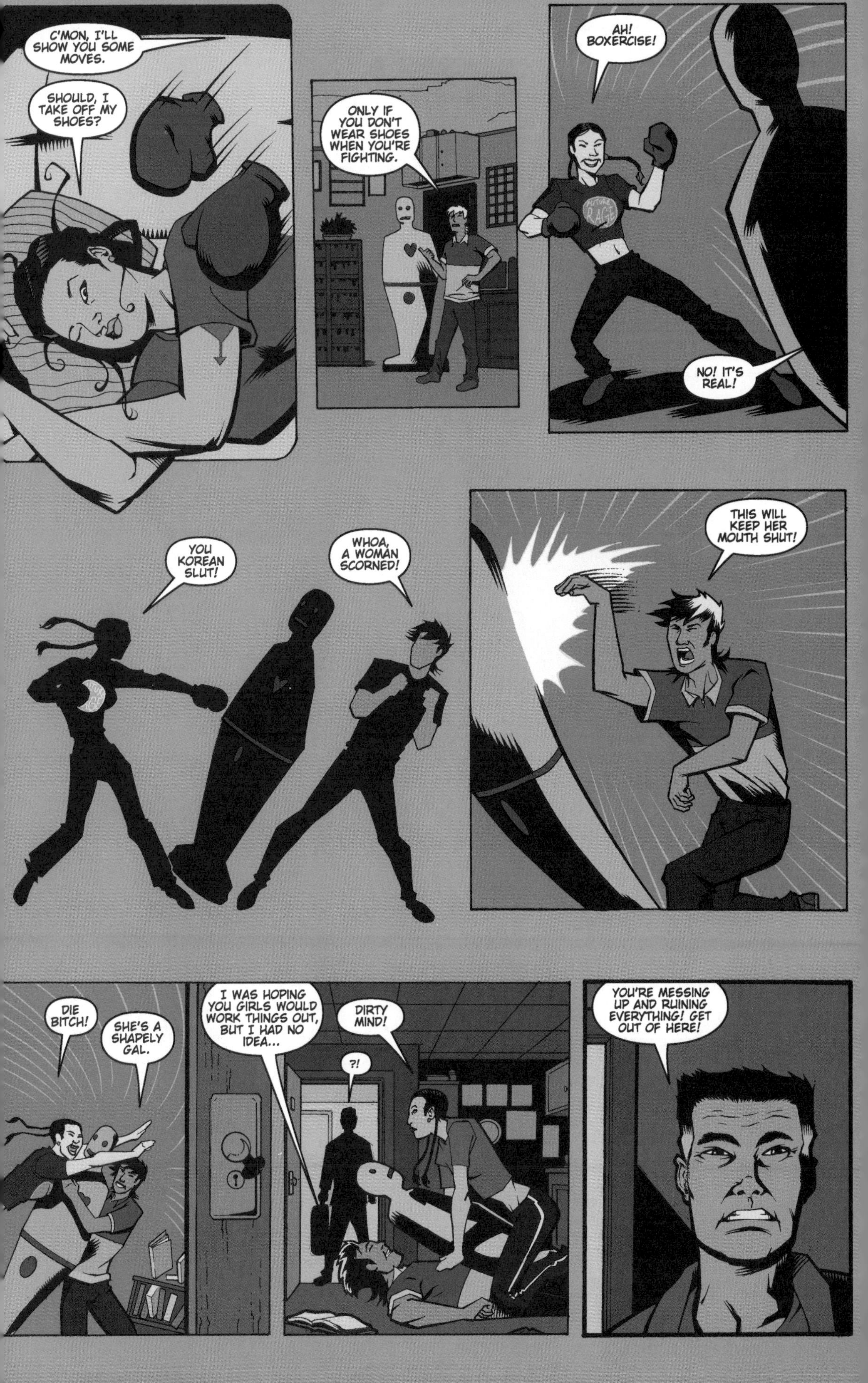
C'MON, I'LL SHOW YOU SOME MOVES.
SHOULD, I TAKE OFF MY SHOES?
ONLY IF YOU DON'T WEAR SHOES WHEN YOU'RE FIGHTING.
AH! BOXERCISE!
NO! IT'S REAL!
YOU KOREAN SLUT!
WHOA, A WOMAN SCORNED!
THIS WILL KEEP HER MOUTH SHUT!
DIE BITCH!
SHE'S A SHAPELY GAL.
I WAS HOPING YOU GIRLS WOULD WORK THINGS OUT, BUT I HAD NO IDEA...
DIRTY MIND!
?!
YOU'RE MESSING UP AND RUINING EVERYTHING! GET OUT OF HERE!

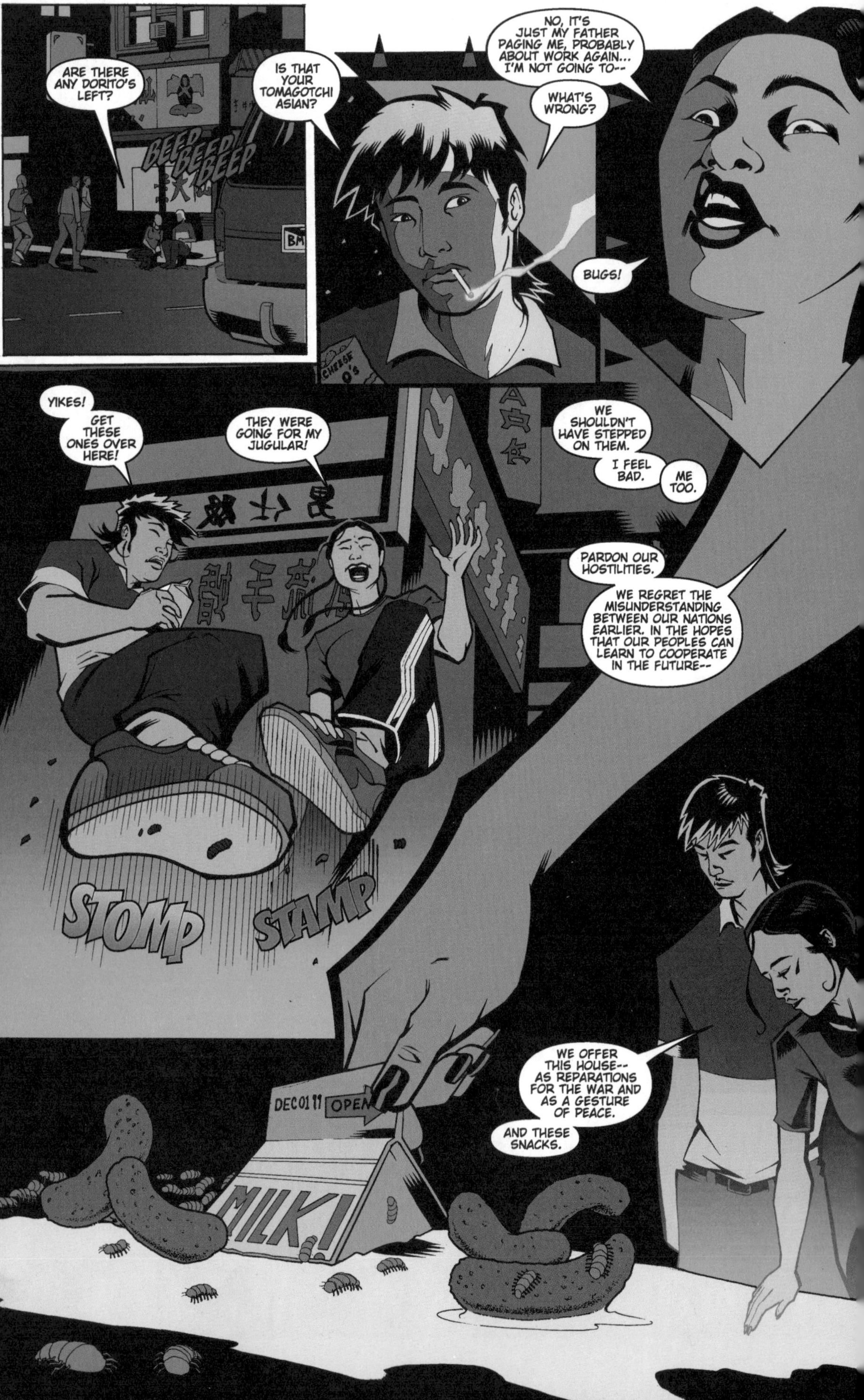
ARE THERE ANY DORITO'S LEFT?
BEEP BEEP BEEP
IS THAT YOUR TOMAGOTCHI ASIAN?
NO, IT'S JUST MY FATHER PAGING ME, PROBABLY ABOUT WORK AGAIN... I'M NOT GOING TO--
WHAT'S WRONG?
BUGS!
YIKES! GET THESE ONES OVER HERE!
THEY WERE GOING FOR MY JUGULAR!
STOMP
STAMP
WE SHOULDN'T HAVE STEPPED ON THEM.
I FEEL BAD.
ME TOO.
PARDON OUR HOSTILITIES.
WE REGRET THE MISUNDERSTANDING BETWEEN OUR NATIONS EARLIER. IN THE HOPES THAT OUR PEOPLES CAN LEARN TO COOPERATE IN THE FUTURE--
WE OFFER THIS HOUSE-- AS REPARATIONS FOR THE WAR AND AS A GESTURE OF PEACE.
AND THESE SNACKS.
DEC01 99
OPEN
MILK!

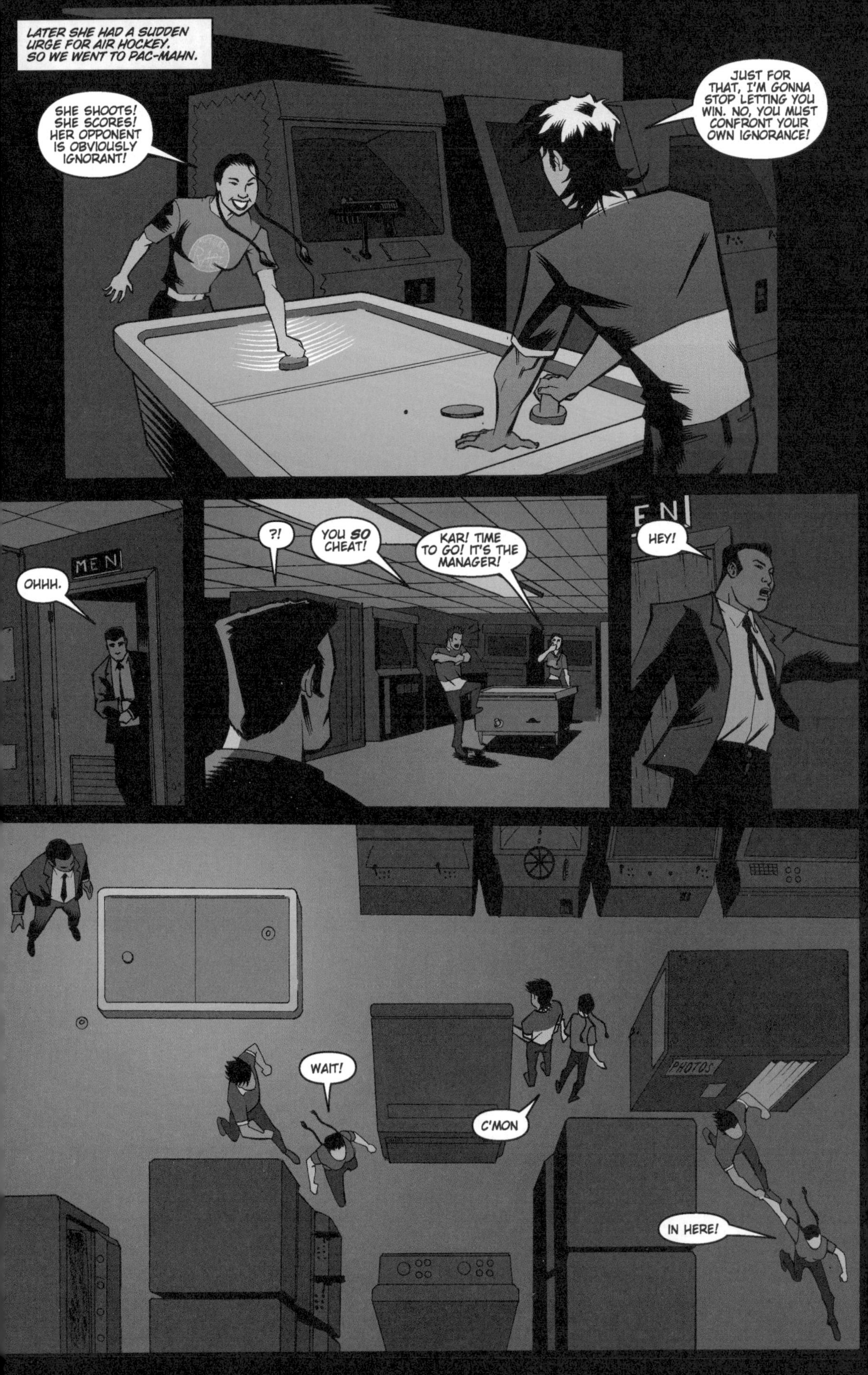
LATER SHE HAD A SUDDEN URGE FOR AIR HOCKEY. SO WE WENT TO PAC-MAHN.
SHE SHOOTS! SHE SCORES! HER OPPONENT IS OBVIOUSLY IGNORANT!
JUST FOR THAT, I'M GONNA STOP LETTING YOU WIN. NO, YOU MUST CONFRONT YOUR OWN IGNORANCE!
MEN
OHHH.
?!
YOU SO CHEAT!
KAR! TIME TO GO! IT'S THE MANAGER!
HEY!
WAIT!
C'MON
PHOTOS
IN HERE!

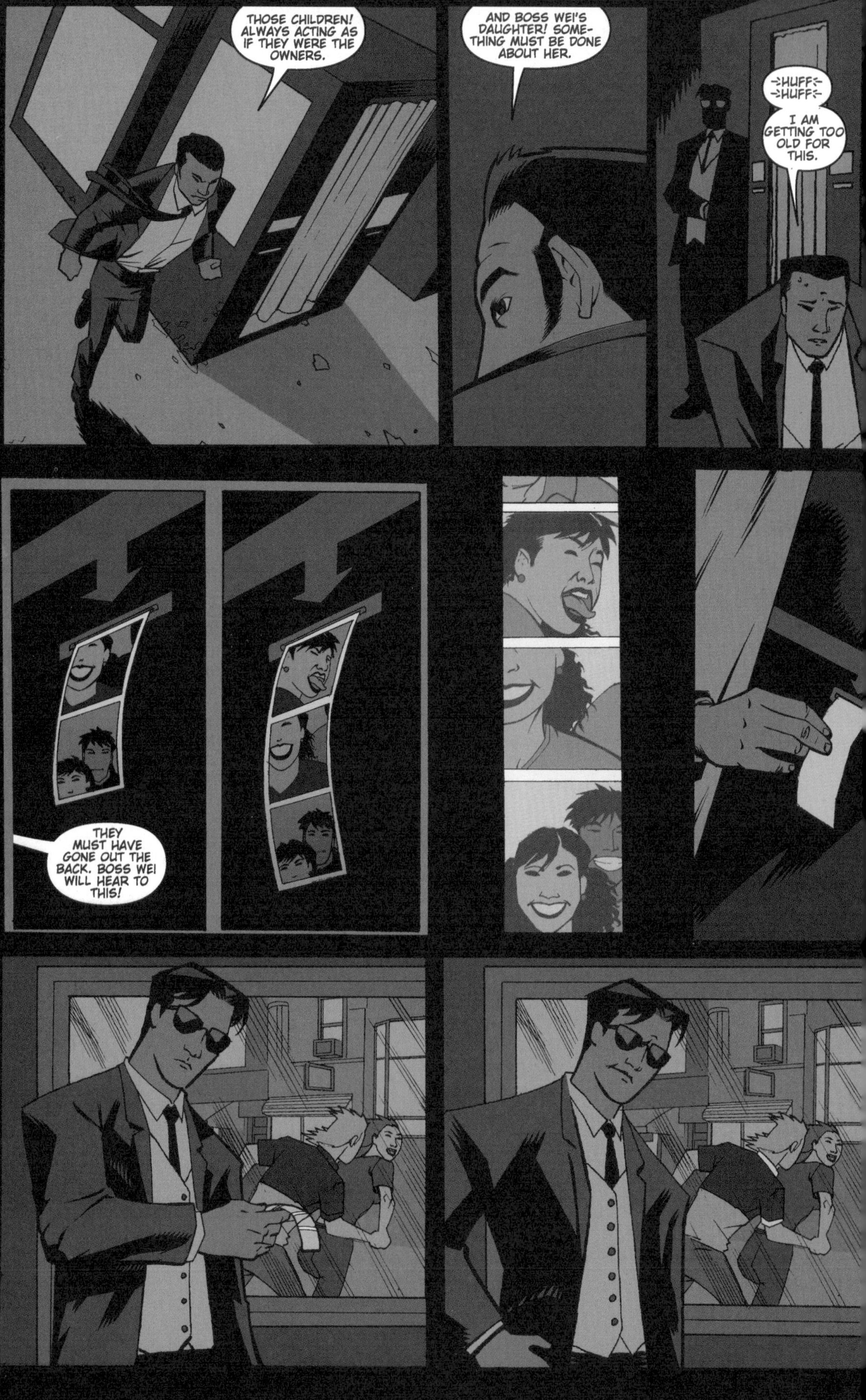
THOSE CHILDREN! ALWAYS ACTING AS IF THEY WERE THE OWNERS.
AND BOSS WEI'S DAUGHTER! SOMETHING MUST BE DONE ABOUT HER.
HUFF HUFF
I AM GETTING TOO OLD FOR THIS.
THEY MUST HAVE GONE OUT THE BACK. BOSS WEI WILL HEAR TO THIS!

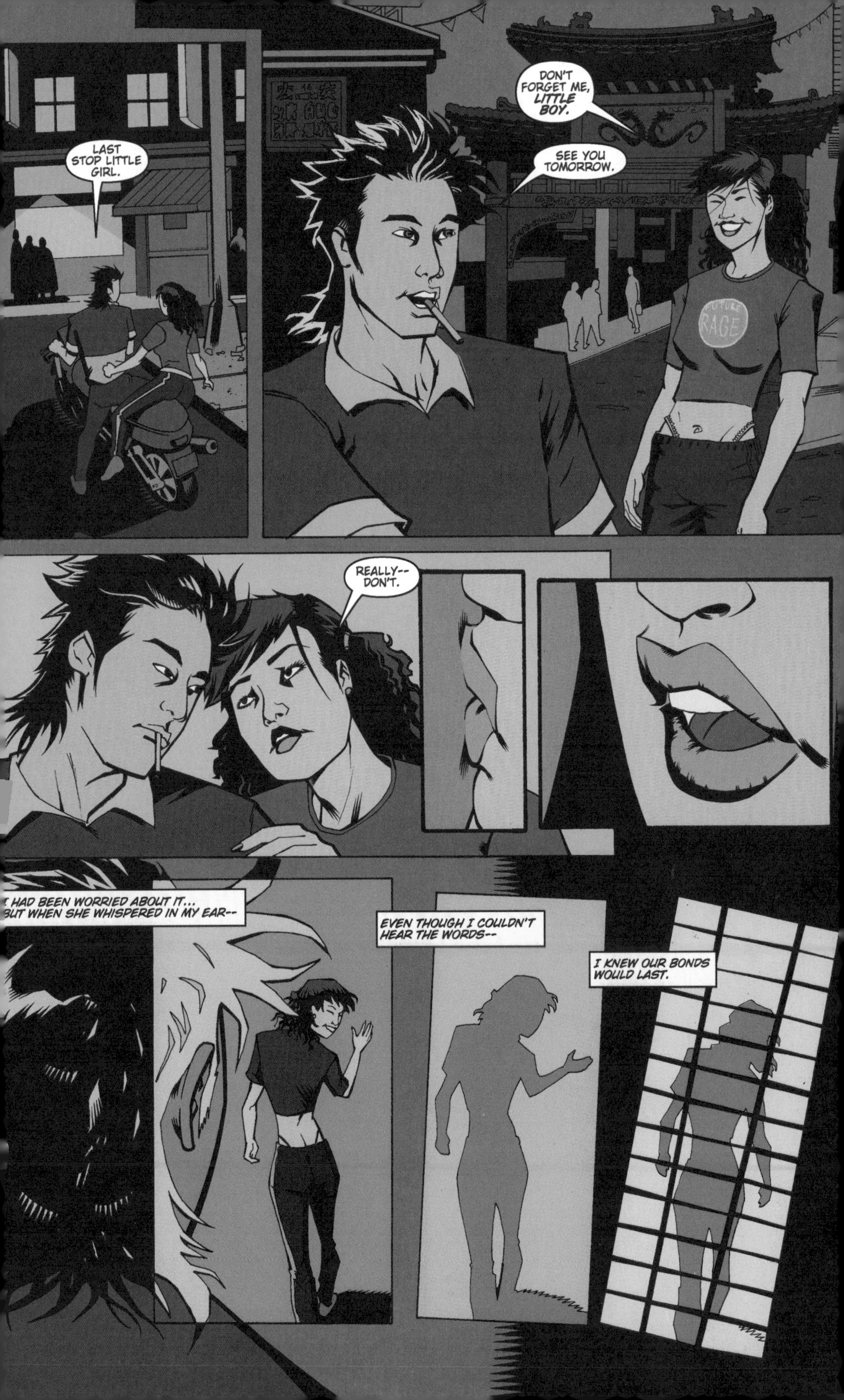

LAST STOP LITTLE GIRL.
DON'T FORGET ME, *LITTLE BOY.*
SEE YOU TOMORROW.
REALLY-- DON'T.
I HAD BEEN WORRIED ABOUT IT... BUT WHEN SHE WHISPERED IN MY EAR--
EVEN THOUGH I COULDN'T HEAR THE WORDS--
I KNEW OUR BONDS WOULD LAST.

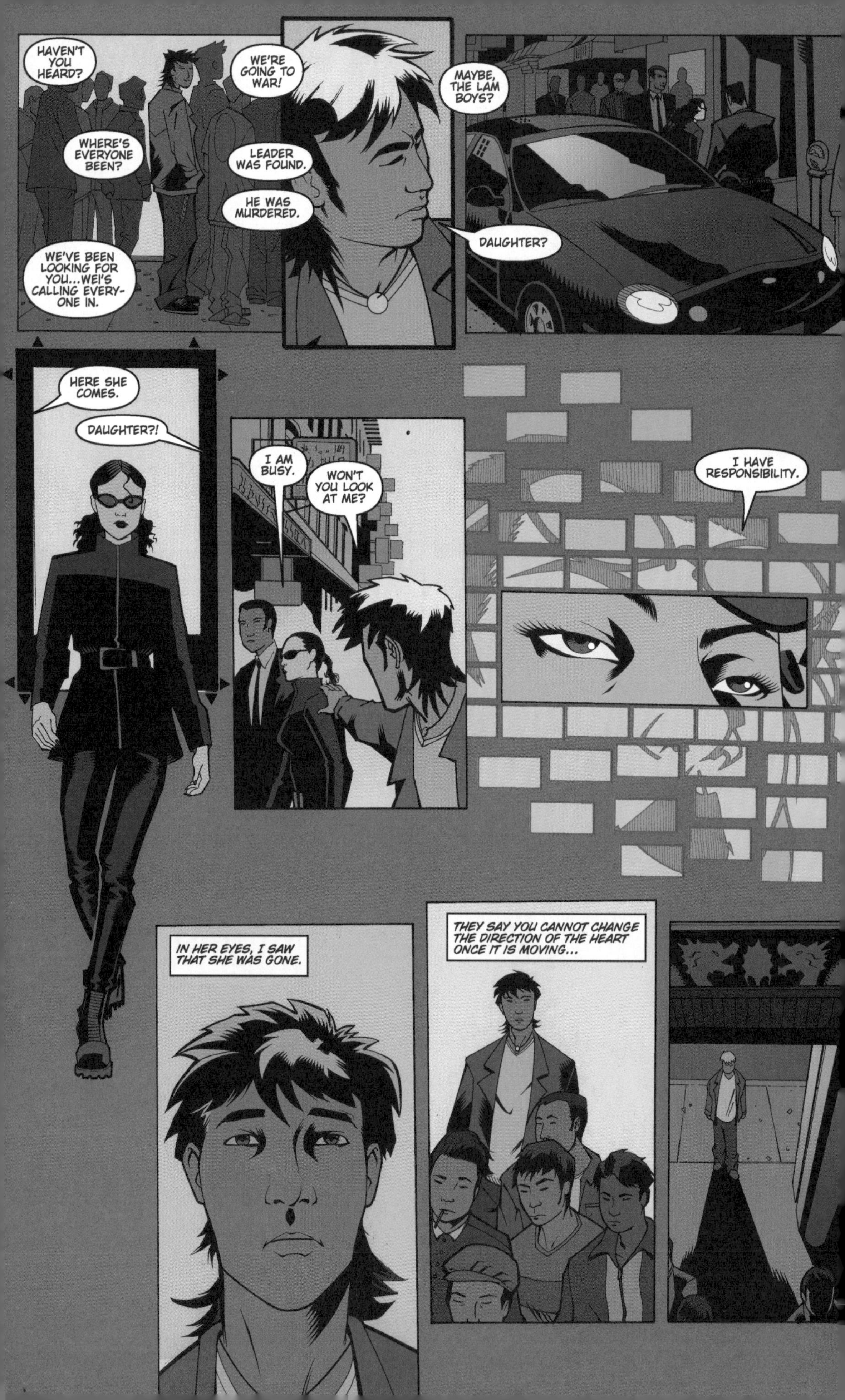
HAVEN'T YOU HEARD?
WHERE'S EVERYONE BEEN?
WE'VE BEEN LOOKING FOR YOU...WEI'S CALLING EVERY-ONE IN.
WE'RE GOING TO WAR!
LEADER WAS FOUND.
HE WAS MURDERED.
MAYBE, THE LAM BOYS?
DAUGHTER?
HERE SHE COMES.
DAUGHTER?!
I AM BUSY.
WON'T YOU LOOK AT ME?
I HAVE RESPONSIBILITY.
IN HER EYES, I SAW THAT SHE WAS GONE.
THEY SAY YOU CANNOT CHANGE THE DIRECTION OF THE HEART ONCE IT IS MOVING...

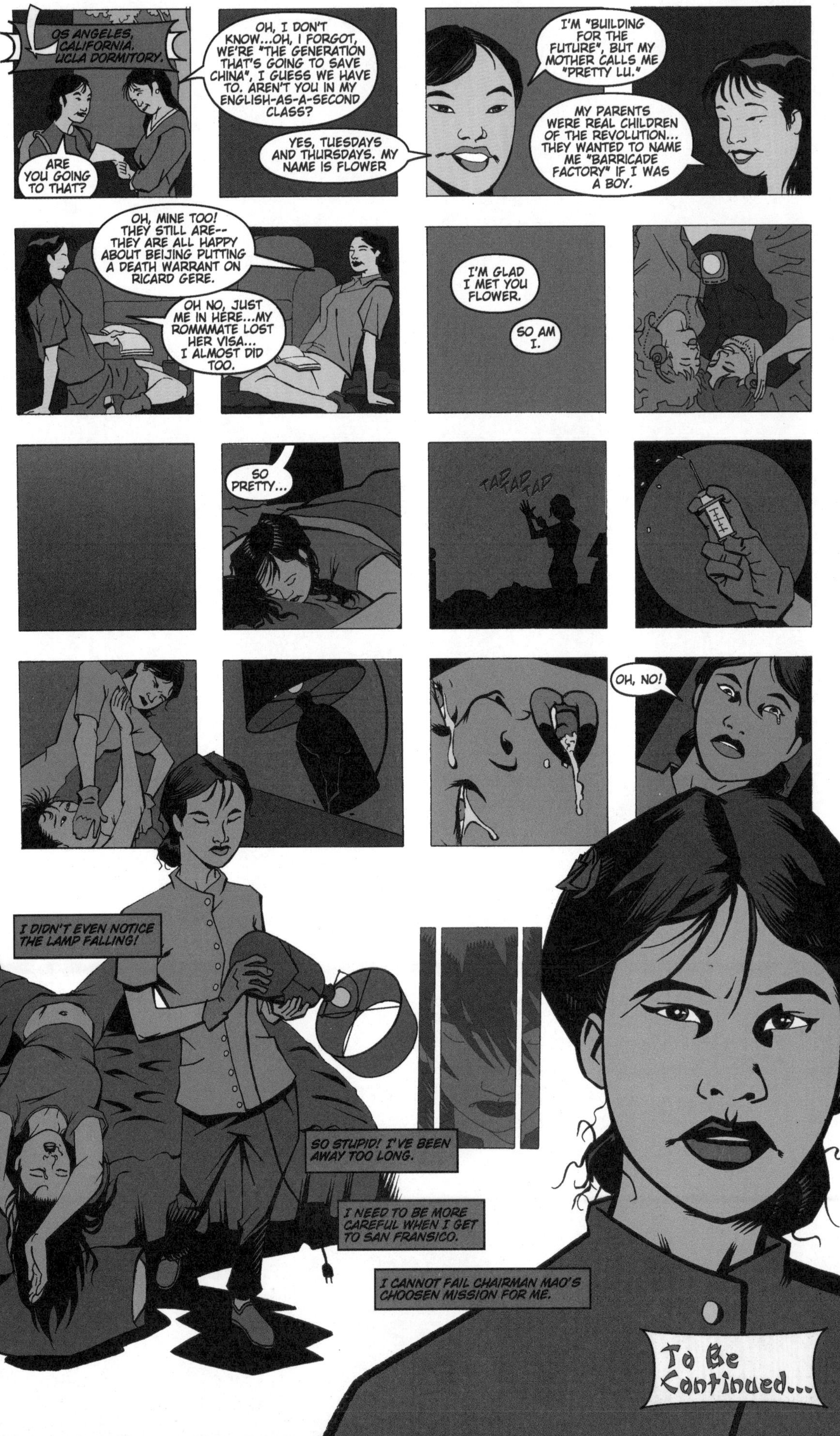
LOS ANGELES, CALIFORNIA. UCLA DORMITORY.
ARE YOU GOING TO THAT?
OH, I DON'T KNOW...OH, I FORGOT, WE'RE "THE GENERATION THAT'S GOING TO SAVE CHINA", I GUESS WE HAVE TO. AREN'T YOU IN MY ENGLISH-AS-A-SECOND CLASS?
YES, TUESDAYS AND THURSDAYS. MY NAME IS FLOWER
I'M "BUILDING FOR THE FUTURE", BUT MY MOTHER CALLS ME "PRETTY LU."
MY PARENTS WERE REAL CHILDREN OF THE REVOLUTION... THEY WANTED TO NAME ME "BARRICADE FACTORY" IF I WAS A BOY.
OH, MINE TOO! THEY STILL ARE-- THEY ARE ALL HAPPY ABOUT BEIJING PUTTING A DEATH WARRANT ON RICARD GERE.
OH NO, JUST ME IN HERE...MY ROMMMATE LOST HER VISA... I ALMOST DID TOO.
I'M GLAD I MET YOU FLOWER.
SO AM I.
SO PRETTY...
TAP TAP TAP
OH, NO!
I DIDN'T EVEN NOTICE THE LAMP FALLING!
SO STUPID! I'VE BEEN AWAY TOO LONG.
I NEED TO BE MORE CAREFUL WHEN I GET TO SAN FRANSICO.
I CANNOT FAIL CHAIRMAN MAO'S CHOOSEN MISSION FOR ME.
To Be Continued...

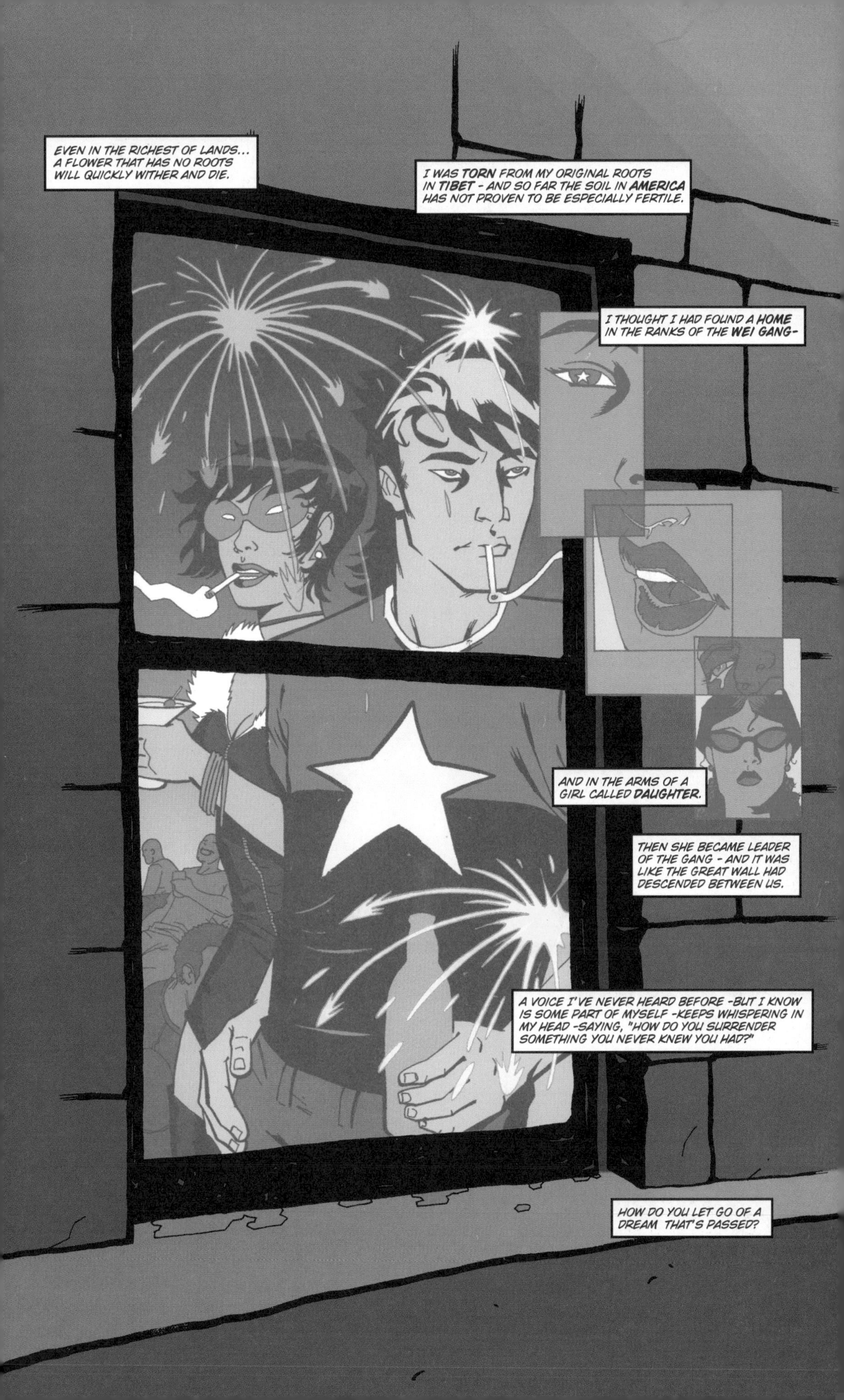
EVEN IN THE RICHEST OF LANDS... A FLOWER THAT HAS NO ROOTS WILL QUICKLY WITHER AND DIE.
I WAS TORN FROM MY ORIGINAL ROOTS IN TIBET - AND SO FAR THE SOIL IN AMERICA HAS NOT PROVEN TO BE ESPECIALLY FERTILE.
I THOUGHT I HAD FOUND A HOME IN THE RANKS OF THE WEI GANG-
AND IN THE ARMS OF A GIRL CALLED DAUGHTER.
THEN SHE BECAME LEADER OF THE GANG - AND IT WAS LIKE THE GREAT WALL HAD DESCENDED BETWEEN US.
A VOICE I'VE NEVER HEARD BEFORE -BUT I KNOW IS SOME PART OF MYSELF -KEEPS WHISPERING IN MY HEAD -SAYING, "HOW DO YOU SURRENDER SOMETHING YOU NEVER KNEW YOU HAD?"
HOW DO YOU LET GO OF A DREAM THAT'S PASSED?

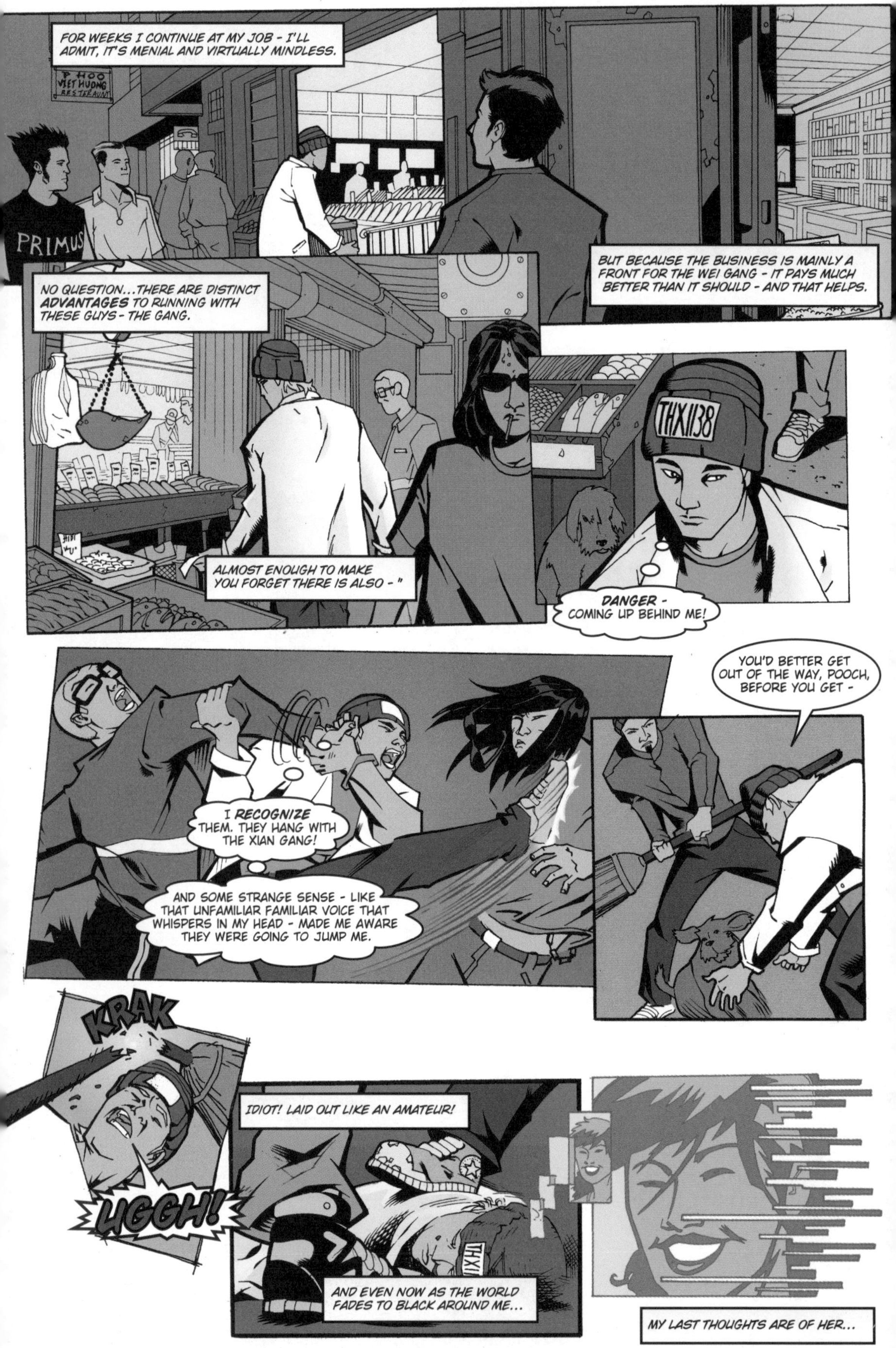

FOR WEEKS I CONTINUE AT MY JOB - I'LL ADMIT, IT'S MENIAL AND VIRTUALLY MINDLESS.
PHOO VIET HUONG RESTERAUNT
PRIMUS
BUT BECAUSE THE BUSINESS IS MAINLY A FRONT FOR THE WEI GANG - IT PAYS MUCH BETTER THAN IT SHOULD - AND THAT HELPS.
NO QUESTION...THERE ARE DISTINCT ADVANTAGES TO RUNNING WITH THESE GUYS - THE GANG.
ALMOST ENOUGH TO MAKE YOU FORGET THERE IS ALSO - "
THX1138
DANGER - COMING UP BEHIND ME!
I RECOGNIZE THEM. THEY HANG WITH THE XIAN GANG!
AND SOME STRANGE SENSE - LIKE THAT UNFAMILIAR FAMILIAR VOICE THAT WHISPERS IN MY HEAD - MADE ME AWARE THEY WERE GOING TO JUMP ME.
YOU'D BETTER GET OUT OF THE WAY, POOCH, BEFORE YOU GET -
KRAK
UGGH!
IDIOT! LAID OUT LIKE AN AMATEUR!
AND EVEN NOW AS THE WORLD FADES TO BLACK AROUND ME...
MY LAST THOUGHTS ARE OF HER...

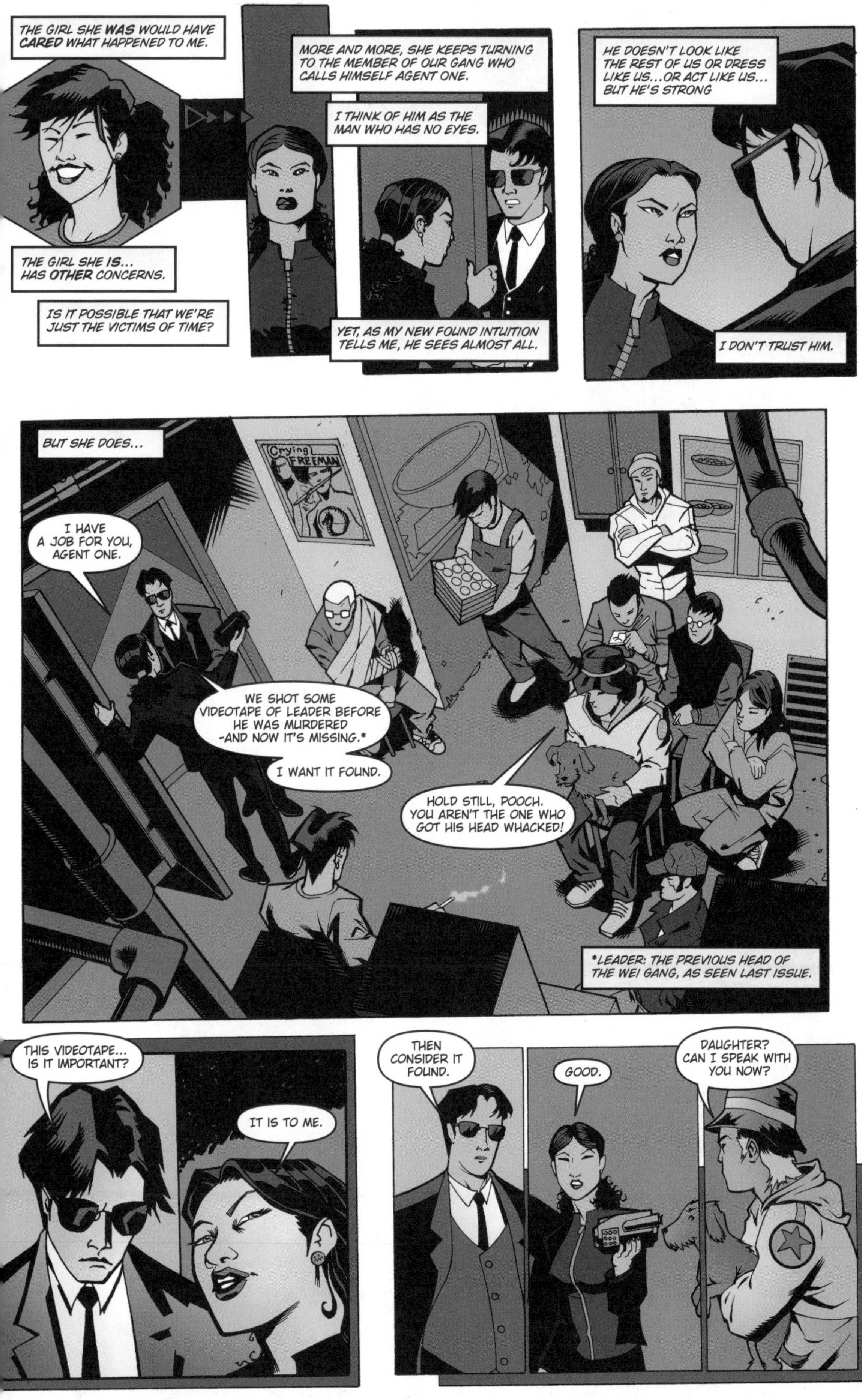
THE GIRL SHE WAS WOULD HAVE CARED WHAT HAPPENED TO ME.
THE GIRL SHE IS... HAS OTHER CONCERNS.
IS IT POSSIBLE THAT WE'RE JUST THE VICTIMS OF TIME?
MORE AND MORE, SHE KEEPS TURNING TO THE MEMBER OF OUR GANG WHO CALLS HIMSELF AGENT ONE.
I THINK OF HIM AS THE MAN WHO HAS NO EYES.
YET, AS MY NEW FOUND INTUITION TELLS ME, HE SEES ALMOST ALL.
HE DOESN'T LOOK LIKE THE REST OF US OR DRESS LIKE US...OR ACT LIKE US... BUT HE'S STRONG
I DON'T TRUST HIM.
BUT SHE DOES...
Crying FREEMAN
I HAVE A JOB FOR YOU, AGENT ONE.
WE SHOT SOME VIDEOTAPE OF LEADER BEFORE HE WAS MURDERED -AND NOW IT'S MISSING.*
I WANT IT FOUND.
HOLD STILL, POOCH. YOU AREN'T THE ONE WHO GOT HIS HEAD WHACKED!
*LEADER: THE PREVIOUS HEAD OF THE WEI GANG, AS SEEN LAST ISSUE.
THIS VIDEOTAPE... IS IT IMPORTANT?
IT IS TO ME.
THEN CONSIDER IT FOUND.
GOOD.
DAUGHTER? CAN I SPEAK WITH YOU NOW?

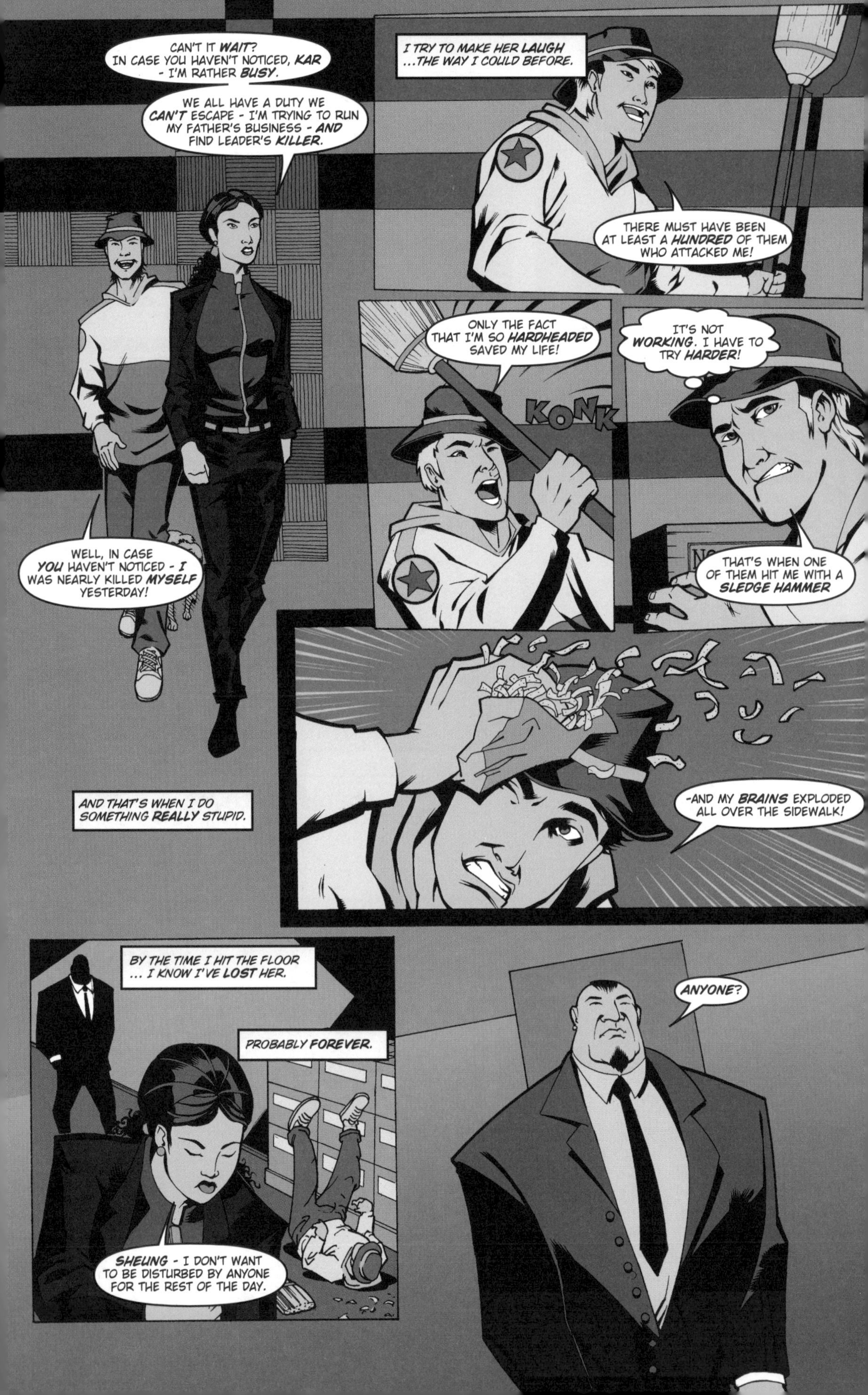
CAN'T IT WAIT? IN CASE YOU HAVEN'T NOTICED, KAR - I'M RATHER BUSY.
WE ALL HAVE A DUTY WE CAN'T ESCAPE - I'M TRYING TO RUN MY FATHER'S BUSINESS - AND FIND LEADER'S KILLER.
WELL, IN CASE YOU HAVEN'T NOTICED - I WAS NEARLY KILLED MYSELF YESTERDAY!
I TRY TO MAKE HER LAUGH ...THE WAY I COULD BEFORE.
THERE MUST HAVE BEEN AT LEAST A HUNDRED OF THEM WHO ATTACKED ME!
ONLY THE FACT THAT I'M SO HARDHEADED SAVED MY LIFE!
KONK
IT'S NOT WORKING. I HAVE TO TRY HARDER!
THAT'S WHEN ONE OF THEM HIT ME WITH A SLEDGE HAMMER
AND THAT'S WHEN I DO SOMETHING REALLY STUPID.
-AND MY BRAINS EXPLODED ALL OVER THE SIDEWALK!
BY THE TIME I HIT THE FLOOR ... I KNOW I'VE LOST HER.
PROBABLY FOREVER.
SHEUNG - I DON'T WANT TO BE DISTURBED BY ANYONE FOR THE REST OF THE DAY.
ANYONE?

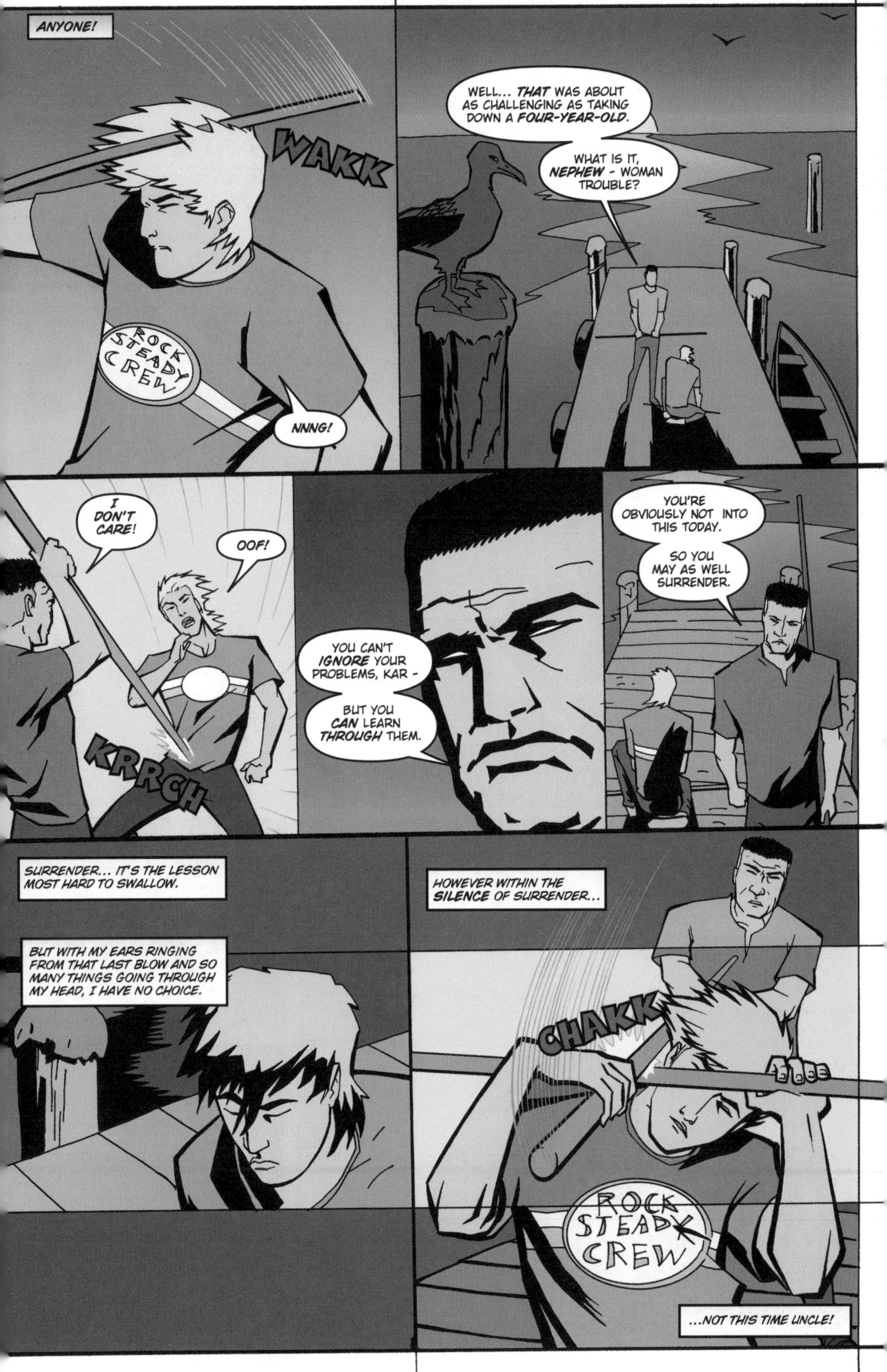
ANYONE!
WAKK
NNNG!
ROCK STEADY CREW
WELL... THAT WAS ABOUT AS CHALLENGING AS TAKING DOWN A FOUR-YEAR-OLD.
WHAT IS IT, NEPHEW - WOMAN TROUBLE?
I DON'T CARE!
OOF!
KRRCH
YOU CAN'T IGNORE YOUR PROBLEMS, KAR -
BUT YOU CAN LEARN THROUGH THEM.
YOU'RE OBVIOUSLY NOT INTO THIS TODAY.
SO YOU MAY AS WELL SURRENDER.
SURRENDER... IT'S THE LESSON MOST HARD TO SWALLOW.
BUT WITH MY EARS RINGING FROM THAT LAST BLOW AND SO MANY THINGS GOING THROUGH MY HEAD, I HAVE NO CHOICE.
HOWEVER WITHIN THE SILENCE OF SURRENDER...
CHAKK
ROCK STEADY CREW
...NOT THIS TIME UNCLE!

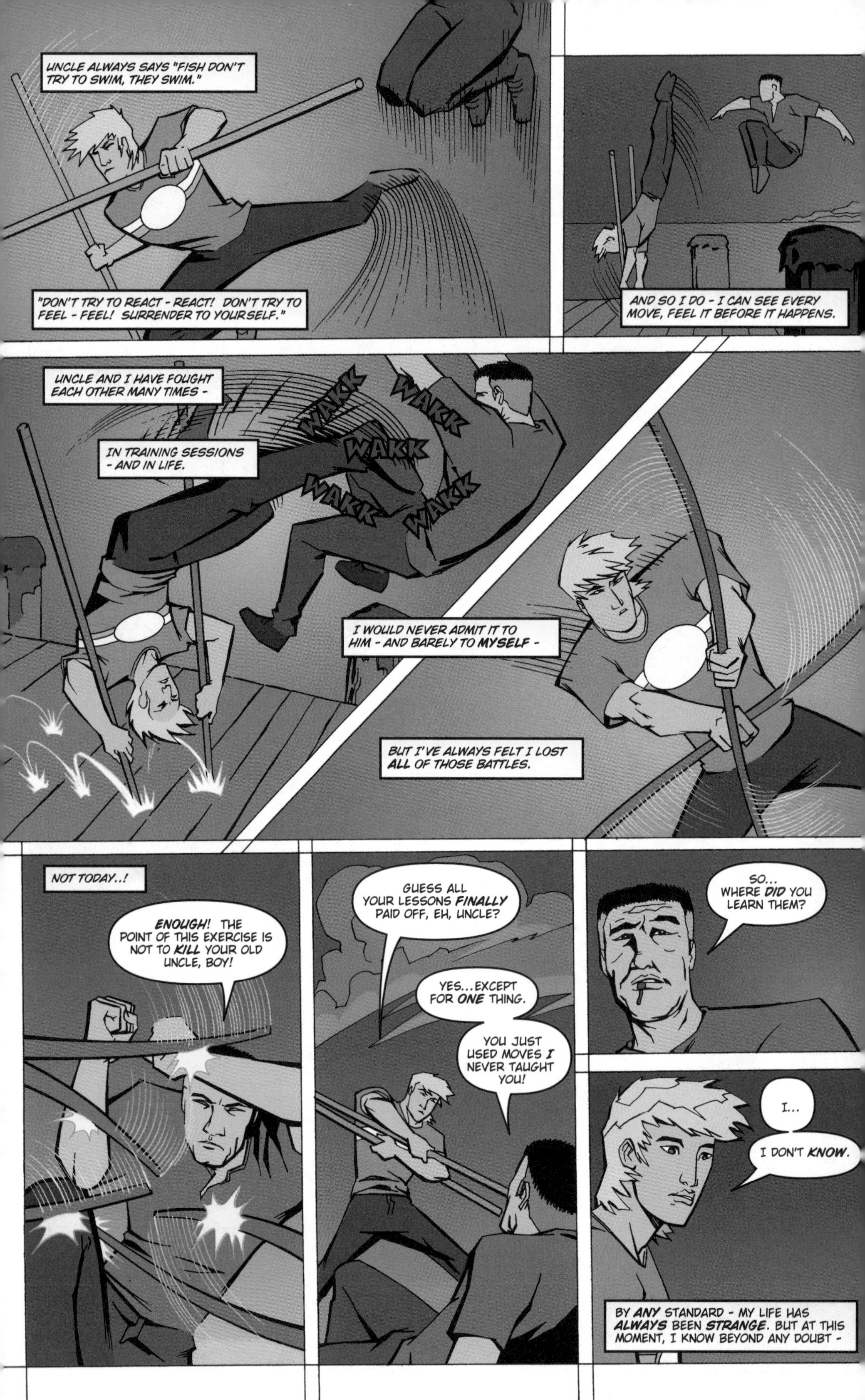
UNCLE ALWAYS SAYS "FISH DON'T TRY TO SWIM, THEY SWIM."
"DON'T TRY TO REACT - REACT! DON'T TRY TO FEEL - FEEL! SURRENDER TO YOURSELF."
AND SO I DO - I CAN SEE EVERY MOVE, FEEL IT BEFORE IT HAPPENS.
UNCLE AND I HAVE FOUGHT EACH OTHER MANY TIMES -
IN TRAINING SESSIONS - AND IN LIFE.
WAKK
WAKK
WAKK
WAKK
WAKK
I WOULD NEVER ADMIT IT TO HIM - AND BARELY TO MYSELF -
BUT I'VE ALWAYS FELT I LOST ALL OF THOSE BATTLES.
NOT TODAY..!
ENOUGH! THE POINT OF THIS EXERCISE IS NOT TO KILL YOUR OLD UNCLE, BOY!
GUESS ALL YOUR LESSONS FINALLY PAID OFF, EH, UNCLE?
YES...EXCEPT FOR ONE THING.
YOU JUST USED MOVES I NEVER TAUGHT YOU!
SO... WHERE DID YOU LEARN THEM?
I...
I DON'T KNOW.
BY ANY STANDARD - MY LIFE HAS ALWAYS BEEN STRANGE. BUT AT THIS MOMENT, I KNOW BEYOND ANY DOUBT -

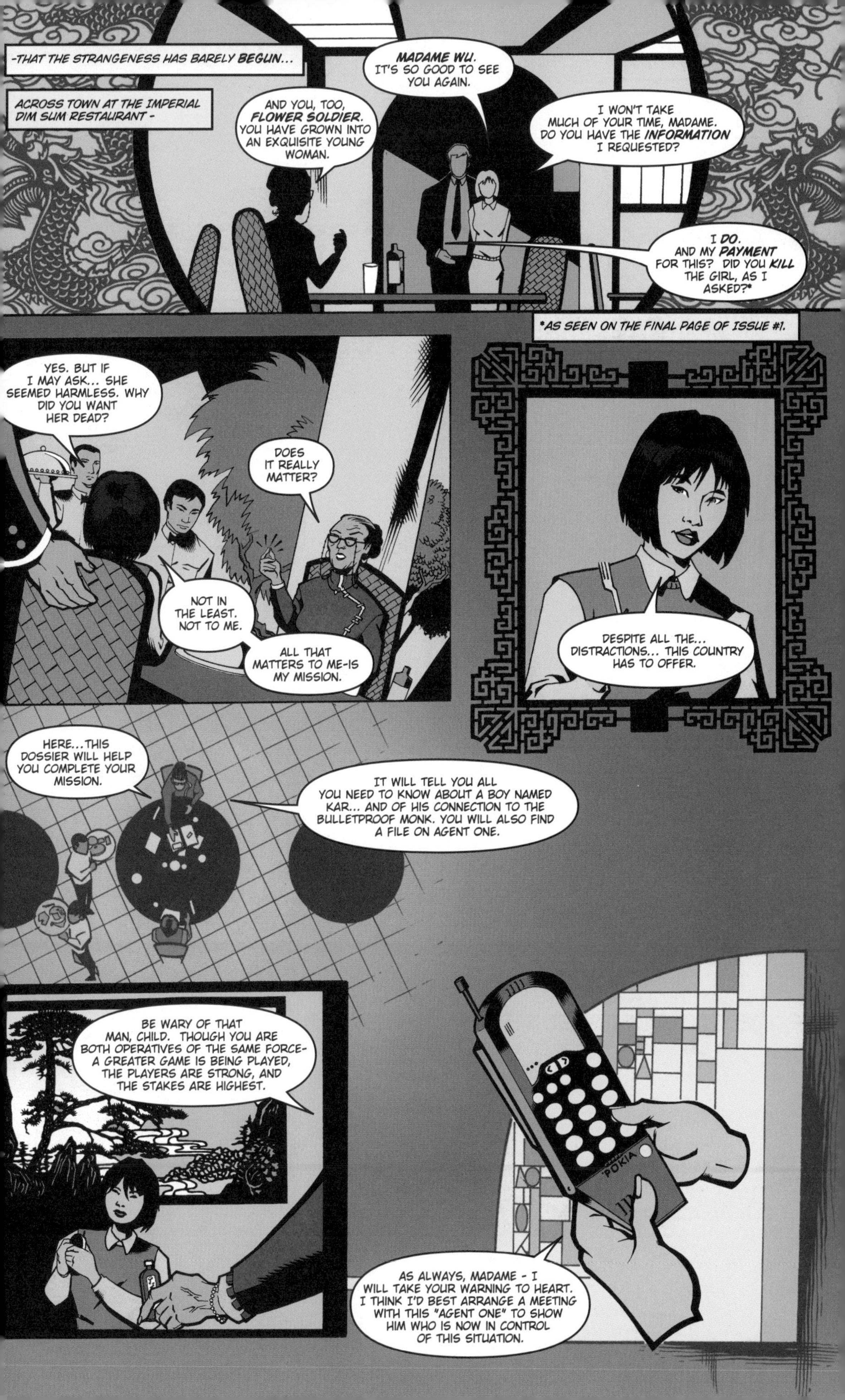
-THAT THE STRANGENESS HAS BARELY BEGUN...
ACROSS TOWN AT THE IMPERIAL DIM SUM RESTAURANT -
MADAME WU. IT'S SO GOOD TO SEE YOU AGAIN.
AND YOU, TOO, FLOWER SOLDIER. YOU HAVE GROWN INTO AN EXQUISITE YOUNG WOMAN.
I WON'T TAKE MUCH OF YOUR TIME, MADAME. DO YOU HAVE THE INFORMATION I REQUESTED?
I DO. AND MY PAYMENT FOR THIS? DID YOU KILL THE GIRL, AS I ASKED?*
*AS SEEN ON THE FINAL PAGE OF ISSUE #1.
YES. BUT IF I MAY ASK... SHE SEEMED HARMLESS. WHY DID YOU WANT HER DEAD?
DOES IT REALLY MATTER?
NOT IN THE LEAST. NOT TO ME.
ALL THAT MATTERS TO ME-IS MY MISSION.
DESPITE ALL THE... DISTRACTIONS... THIS COUNTRY HAS TO OFFER.
HERE...THIS DOSSIER WILL HELP YOU COMPLETE YOUR MISSION.
IT WILL TELL YOU ALL YOU NEED TO KNOW ABOUT A BOY NAMED KAR... AND OF HIS CONNECTION TO THE BULLETPROOF MONK. YOU WILL ALSO FIND A FILE ON AGENT ONE.
BE WARY OF THAT MAN, CHILD. THOUGH YOU ARE BOTH OPERATIVES OF THE SAME FORCE- A GREATER GAME IS BEING PLAYED, THE PLAYERS ARE STRONG, AND THE STAKES ARE HIGHEST.
POKIA
AS ALWAYS, MADAME - I WILL TAKE YOUR WARNING TO HEART. I THINK I'D BEST ARRANGE A MEETING WITH THIS "AGENT ONE" TO SHOW HIM WHO IS NOW IN CONTROL OF THIS SITUATION.

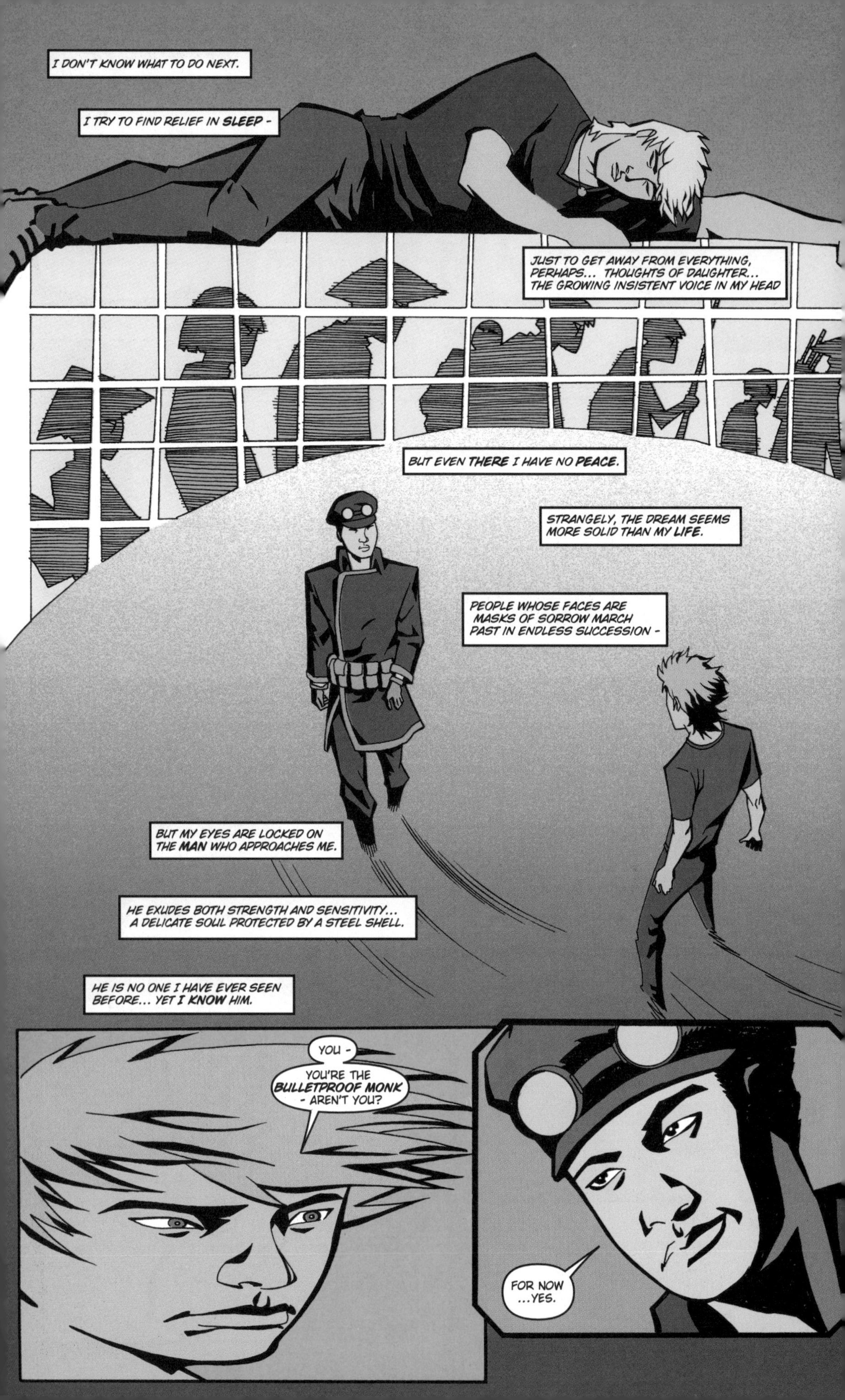
I DON'T KNOW WHAT TO DO NEXT.
I TRY TO FIND RELIEF IN SLEEP -
JUST TO GET AWAY FROM EVERYTHING, PERHAPS... THOUGHTS OF DAUGHTER... THE GROWING INSISTENT VOICE IN MY HEAD
BUT EVEN THERE I HAVE NO PEACE.
STRANGELY, THE DREAM SEEMS MORE SOLID THAN MY LIFE.
PEOPLE WHOSE FACES ARE MASKS OF SORROW MARCH PAST IN ENDLESS SUCCESSION -
BUT MY EYES ARE LOCKED ON THE MAN WHO APPROACHES ME.
HE EXUDES BOTH STRENGTH AND SENSITIVITY... A DELICATE SOUL PROTECTED BY A STEEL SHELL.
HE IS NO ONE I HAVE EVER SEEN BEFORE... YET I KNOW HIM.
YOU -
YOU'RE THE BULLETPROOF MONK - AREN'T YOU?
FOR NOW ...YES.

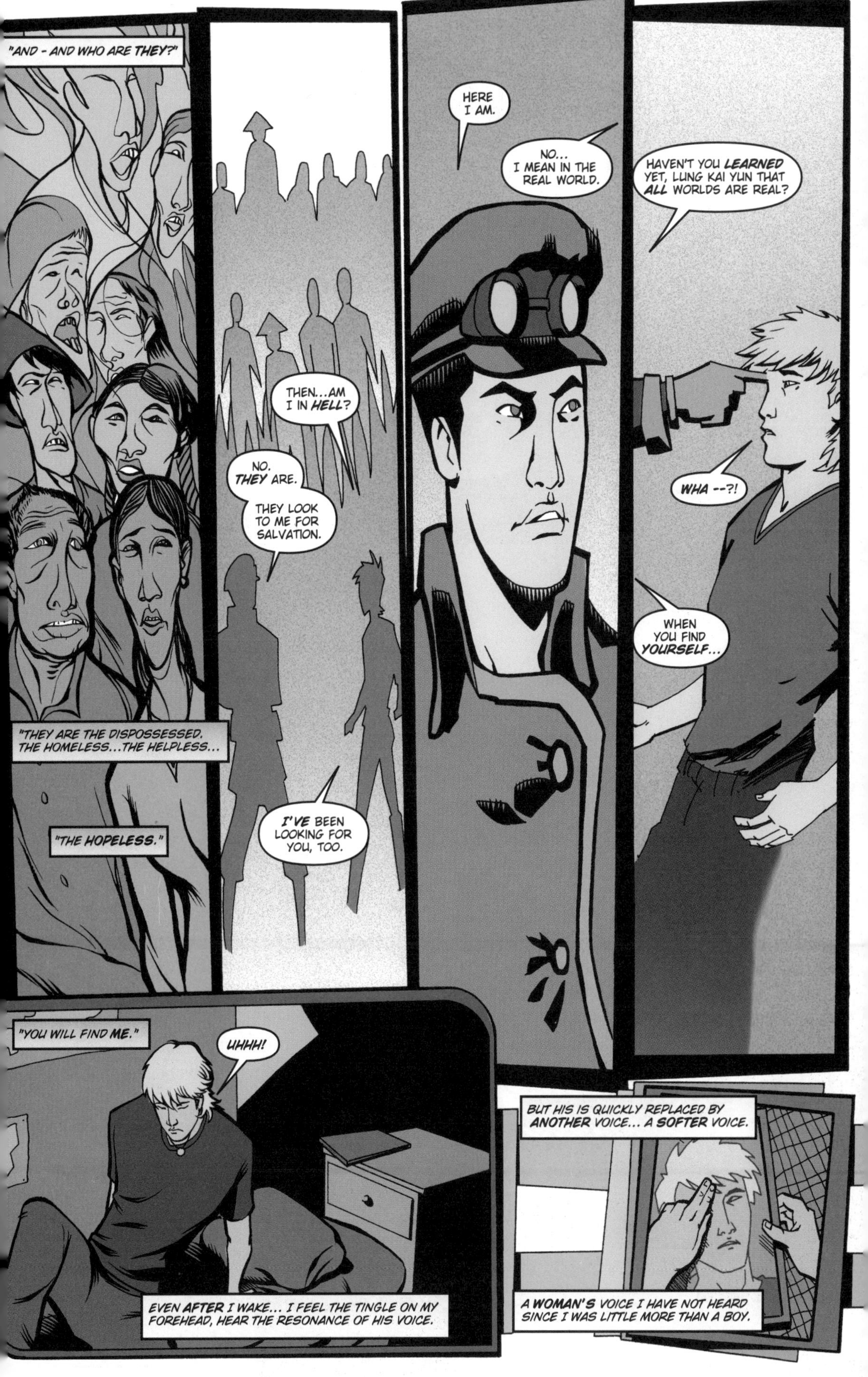
"AND - AND WHO ARE THEY?"
"THEY ARE THE DISPOSSESSED. THE HOMELESS...THE HELPLESS...
"THE HOPELESS."
THEN...AM I IN HELL?
NO. THEY ARE.
THEY LOOK TO ME FOR SALVATION.
I'VE BEEN LOOKING FOR YOU, TOO.
HERE I AM.
NO... I MEAN IN THE REAL WORLD.
HAVEN'T YOU LEARNED YET, LUNG KAI YUN THAT ALL WORLDS ARE REAL?
WHA --?!
WHEN YOU FIND YOURSELF...
"YOU WILL FIND ME."
UHHH!
EVEN AFTER I WAKE... I FEEL THE TINGLE ON MY FOREHEAD, HEAR THE RESONANCE OF HIS VOICE.
BUT HIS IS QUICKLY REPLACED BY ANOTHER VOICE... A SOFTER VOICE.
A WOMAN'S VOICE I HAVE NOT HEARD SINCE I WAS LITTLE MORE THAN A BOY.

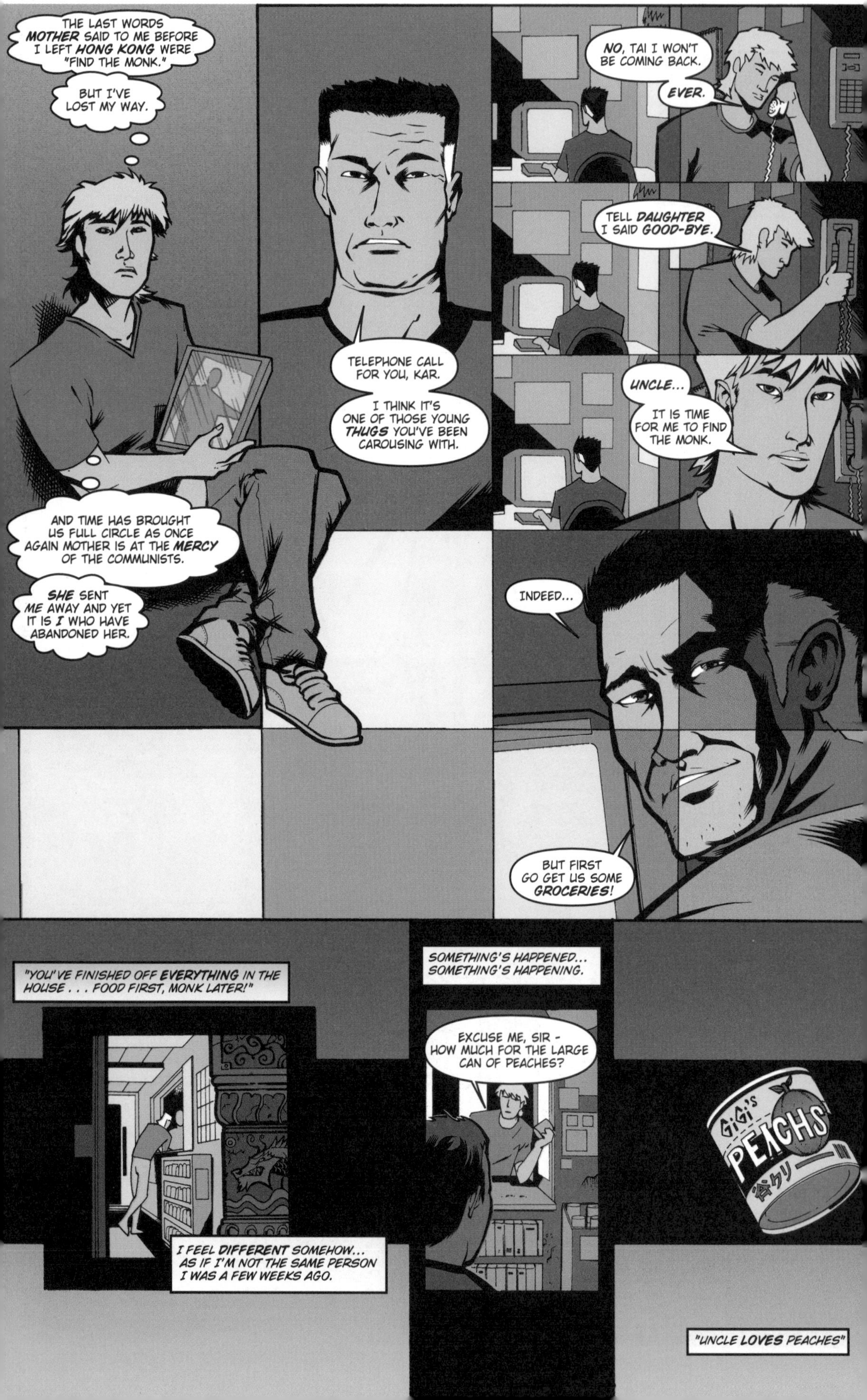
THE LAST WORDS MOTHER SAID TO ME BEFORE I LEFT HONG KONG WERE "FIND THE MONK."
BUT I'VE LOST MY WAY.
TELEPHONE CALL FOR YOU, KAR.
I THINK IT'S ONE OF THOSE YOUNG THUGS YOU'VE BEEN CAROUSING WITH.
NO, TAI I WON'T BE COMING BACK.
EVER.
TELL DAUGHTER I SAID GOOD-BYE.
UNCLE...
IT IS TIME FOR ME TO FIND THE MONK.
AND TIME HAS BROUGHT US FULL CIRCLE AS ONCE AGAIN MOTHER IS AT THE MERCY OF THE COMMUNISTS.
SHE SENT ME AWAY AND YET IT IS I WHO HAVE ABANDONED HER.
INDEED...
BUT FIRST GO GET US SOME GROCERIES!
"YOU'VE FINISHED OFF EVERYTHING IN THE HOUSE . . . FOOD FIRST, MONK LATER!"
I FEEL DIFFERENT SOMEHOW... AS IF I'M NOT THE SAME PERSON I WAS A FEW WEEKS AGO.
SOMETHING'S HAPPENED... SOMETHING'S HAPPENING.
EXCUSE ME, SIR - HOW MUCH FOR THE LARGE CAN OF PEACHES?
GiGi'S
PEACHS
"UNCLE LOVES PEACHES"

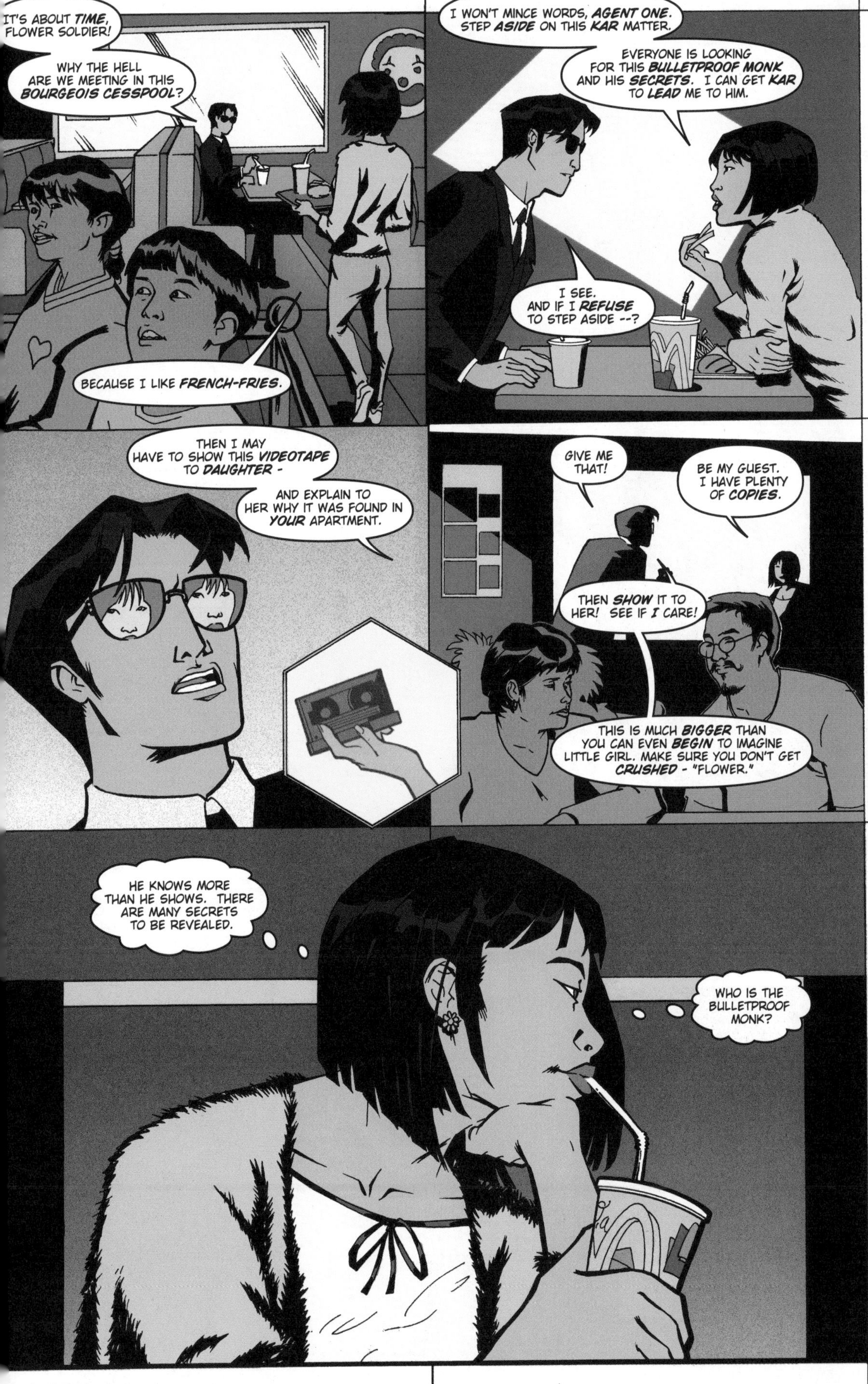
IT'S ABOUT TIME, FLOWER SOLDIER!
WHY THE HELL ARE WE MEETING IN THIS BOURGEOIS CESSPOOL?
BECAUSE I LIKE FRENCH-FRIES.
I WON'T MINCE WORDS, AGENT ONE. STEP ASIDE ON THIS KAR MATTER.
EVERYONE IS LOOKING FOR THIS BULLETPROOF MONK AND HIS SECRETS. I CAN GET KAR TO LEAD ME TO HIM.
I SEE. AND IF I REFUSE TO STEP ASIDE --?
THEN I MAY HAVE TO SHOW THIS VIDEOTAPE TO DAUGHTER -
AND EXPLAIN TO HER WHY IT WAS FOUND IN YOUR APARTMENT.
GIVE ME THAT!
BE MY GUEST. I HAVE PLENTY OF COPIES.
THEN SHOW IT TO HER! SEE IF I CARE!
THIS IS MUCH BIGGER THAN YOU CAN EVEN BEGIN TO IMAGINE LITTLE GIRL. MAKE SURE YOU DON'T GET CRUSHED - "FLOWER."
HE KNOWS MORE THAN HE SHOWS. THERE ARE MANY SECRETS TO BE REVEALED.
WHO IS THE BULLETPROOF MONK?

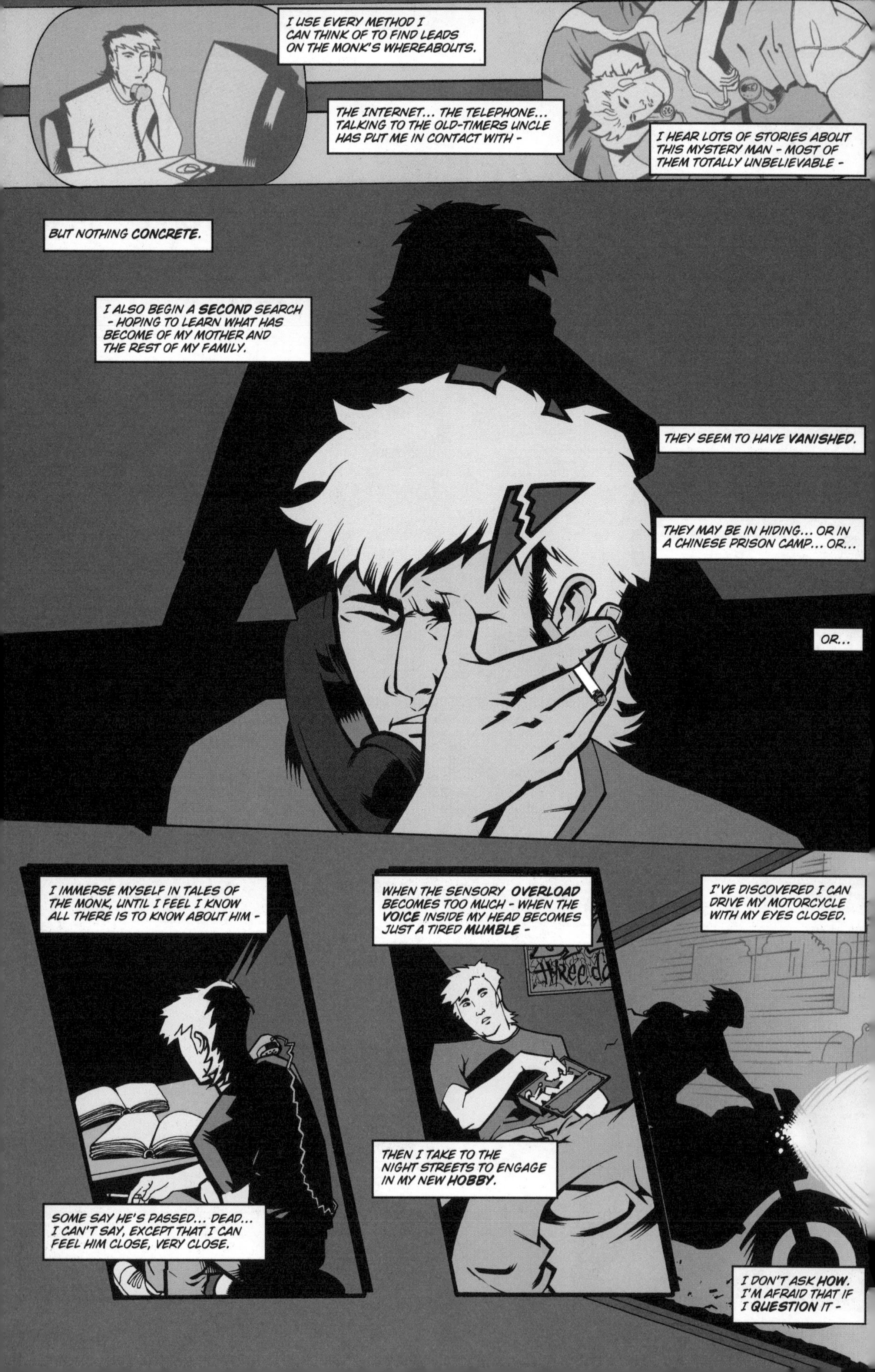
I USE EVERY METHOD I CAN THINK OF TO FIND LEADS ON THE MONK'S WHEREABOUTS.
THE INTERNET... THE TELEPHONE... TALKING TO THE OLD-TIMERS UNCLE HAS PUT ME IN CONTACT WITH -
I HEAR LOTS OF STORIES ABOUT THIS MYSTERY MAN - MOST OF THEM TOTALLY UNBELIEVABLE -
BUT NOTHING CONCRETE.
I ALSO BEGIN A SECOND SEARCH - HOPING TO LEARN WHAT HAS BECOME OF MY MOTHER AND THE REST OF MY FAMILY.
THEY SEEM TO HAVE VANISHED.
THEY MAY BE IN HIDING... OR IN A CHINESE PRISON CAMP... OR...
OR...
I IMMERSE MYSELF IN TALES OF THE MONK, UNTIL I FEEL I KNOW ALL THERE IS TO KNOW ABOUT HIM -
SOME SAY HE'S PASSED... DEAD... I CAN'T SAY, EXCEPT THAT I CAN FEEL HIM CLOSE, VERY CLOSE.
WHEN THE SENSORY OVERLOAD BECOMES TOO MUCH - WHEN THE VOICE INSIDE MY HEAD BECOMES JUST A TIRED MUMBLE -
THEN I TAKE TO THE NIGHT STREETS TO ENGAGE IN MY NEW HOBBY.
I'VE DISCOVERED I CAN DRIVE MY MOTORCYCLE WITH MY EYES CLOSED.
I DON'T ASK HOW. I'M AFRAID THAT IF I QUESTION IT -

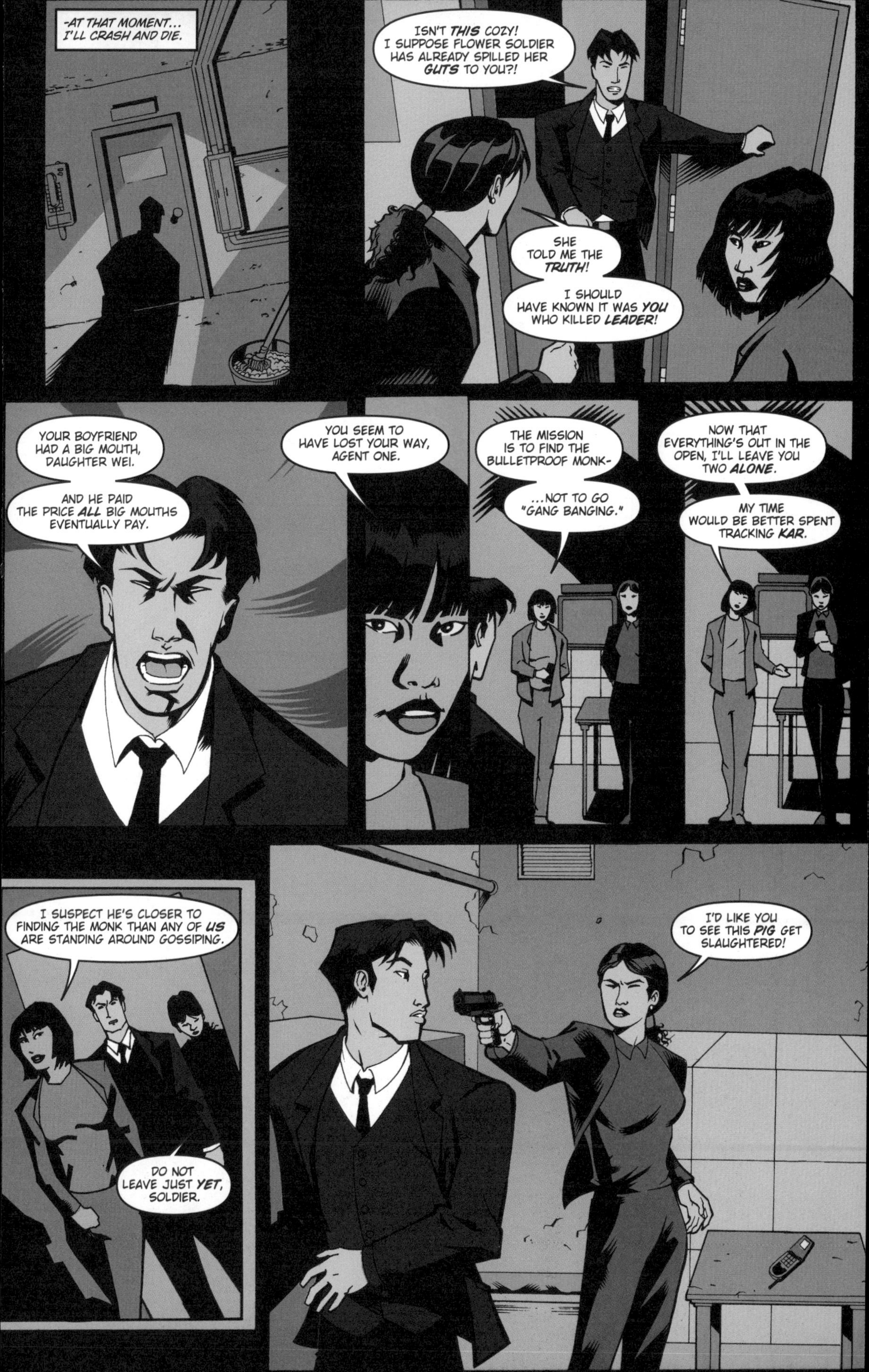
-AT THAT MOMENT... I'LL CRASH AND DIE.
ISN'T THIS COZY! I SUPPOSE FLOWER SOLDIER HAS ALREADY SPILLED HER GUTS TO YOU?!
SHE TOLD ME THE TRUTH!
I SHOULD HAVE KNOWN IT WAS YOU WHO KILLED LEADER!
YOUR BOYFRIEND HAD A BIG MOUTH, DAUGHTER WEI.
AND HE PAID THE PRICE ALL BIG MOUTHS EVENTUALLY PAY.
YOU SEEM TO HAVE LOST YOUR WAY, AGENT ONE.
THE MISSION IS TO FIND THE BULLETPROOF MONK-
...NOT TO GO "GANG BANGING."
NOW THAT EVERYTHING'S OUT IN THE OPEN, I'LL LEAVE YOU TWO ALONE.
MY TIME WOULD BE BETTER SPENT TRACKING KAR.
I SUSPECT HE'S CLOSER TO FINDING THE MONK THAN ANY OF US ARE STANDING AROUND GOSSIPING.
DO NOT LEAVE JUST YET, SOLDIER.
I'D LIKE YOU TO SEE THIS PIG GET SLAUGHTERED!

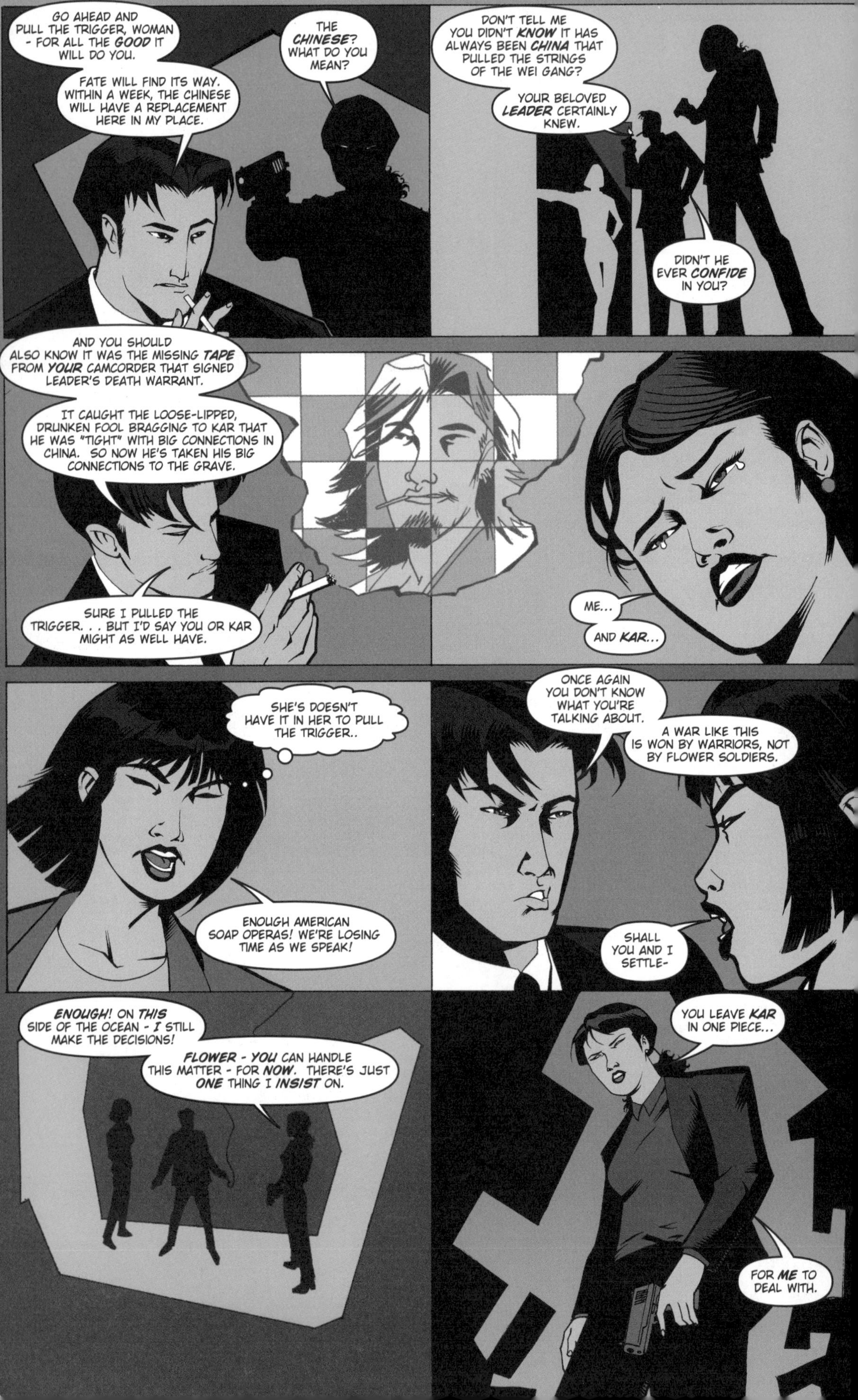
GO AHEAD AND PULL THE TRIGGER, WOMAN - FOR ALL THE GOOD IT WILL DO YOU.
FATE WILL FIND ITS WAY. WITHIN A WEEK, THE CHINESE WILL HAVE A REPLACEMENT HERE IN MY PLACE.
THE CHINESE? WHAT DO YOU MEAN?
DON'T TELL ME YOU DIDN'T KNOW IT HAS ALWAYS BEEN CHINA THAT PULLED THE STRINGS OF THE WEI GANG?
YOUR BELOVED LEADER CERTAINLY KNEW.
DIDN'T HE EVER CONFIDE IN YOU?
AND YOU SHOULD ALSO KNOW IT WAS THE MISSING TAPE FROM YOUR CAMCORDER THAT SIGNED LEADER'S DEATH WARRANT.
IT CAUGHT THE LOOSE-LIPPED, DRUNKEN FOOL BRAGGING TO KAR THAT HE WAS "TIGHT" WITH BIG CONNECTIONS IN CHINA. SO NOW HE'S TAKEN HIS BIG CONNECTIONS TO THE GRAVE.
SURE I PULLED THE TRIGGER. . . BUT I'D SAY YOU OR KAR MIGHT AS WELL HAVE.
ME...
AND KAR...
SHE'S DOESN'T HAVE IT IN HER TO PULL THE TRIGGER..
ENOUGH AMERICAN SOAP OPERAS! WE'RE LOSING TIME AS WE SPEAK!
ONCE AGAIN YOU DON'T KNOW WHAT YOU'RE TALKING ABOUT.
A WAR LIKE THIS IS WON BY WARRIORS, NOT BY FLOWER SOLDIERS.
SHALL YOU AND I SETTLE-
ENOUGH! ON THIS SIDE OF THE OCEAN - I STILL MAKE THE DECISIONS!
FLOWER - YOU CAN HANDLE THIS MATTER - FOR NOW. THERE'S JUST ONE THING I INSIST ON.
YOU LEAVE KAR IN ONE PIECE...
FOR ME TO DEAL WITH.

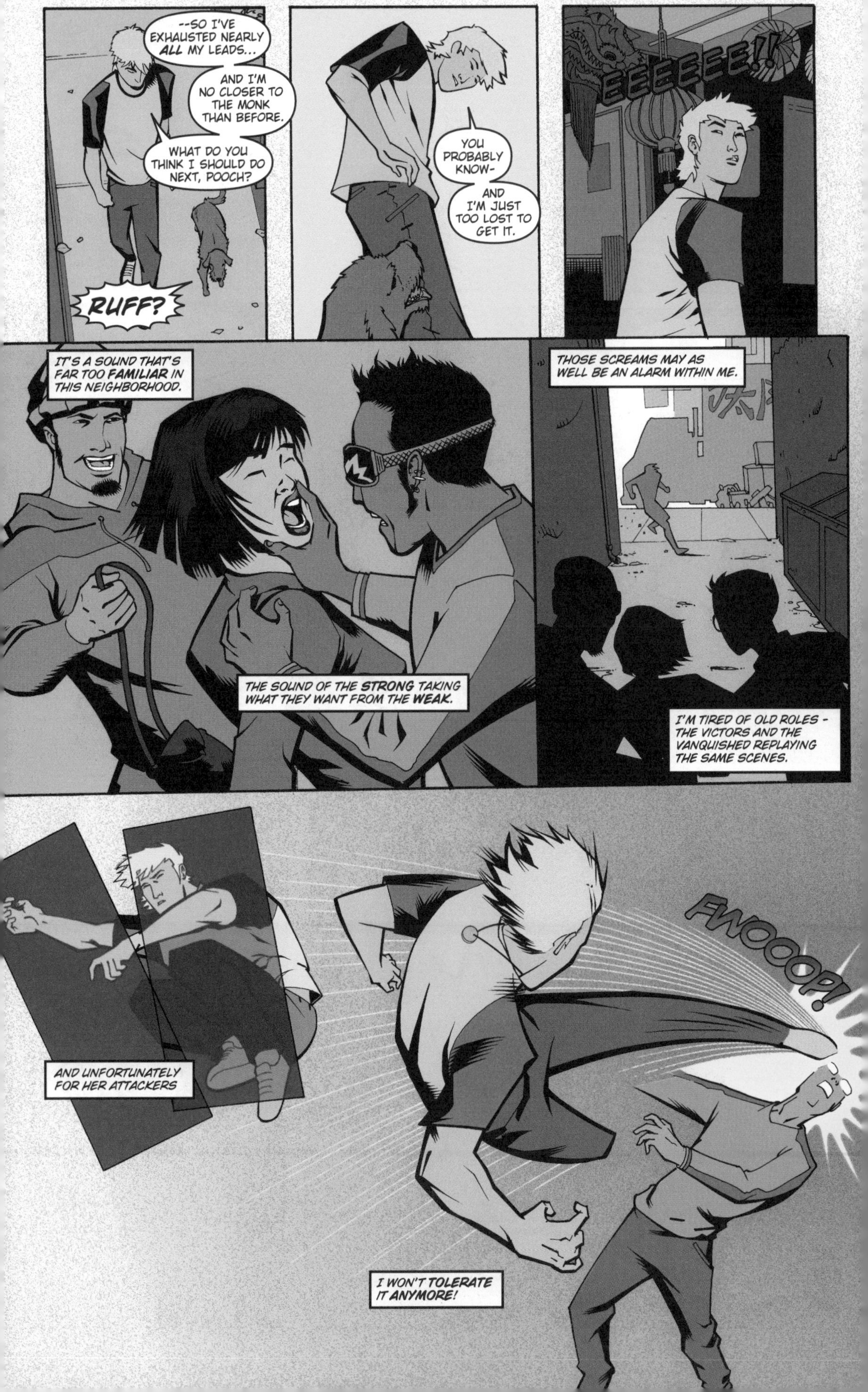
--SO I'VE EXHAUSTED NEARLY ALL MY LEADS...
AND I'M NO CLOSER TO THE MONK THAN BEFORE.
WHAT DO YOU THINK I SHOULD DO NEXT, POOCH?
RUFF?
YOU PROBABLY KNOW-
AND I'M JUST TOO LOST TO GET IT.
EEEEEE!!
IT'S A SOUND THAT'S FAR TOO FAMILIAR IN THIS NEIGHBORHOOD.
THE SOUND OF THE STRONG TAKING WHAT THEY WANT FROM THE WEAK.
THOSE SCREAMS MAY AS WELL BE AN ALARM WITHIN ME.
I'M TIRED OF OLD ROLES - THE VICTORS AND THE VANQUISHED REPLAYING THE SAME SCENES.
AND UNFORTUNATELY FOR HER ATTACKERS
FWOOOP!
I WON'T TOLERATE IT ANYMORE!

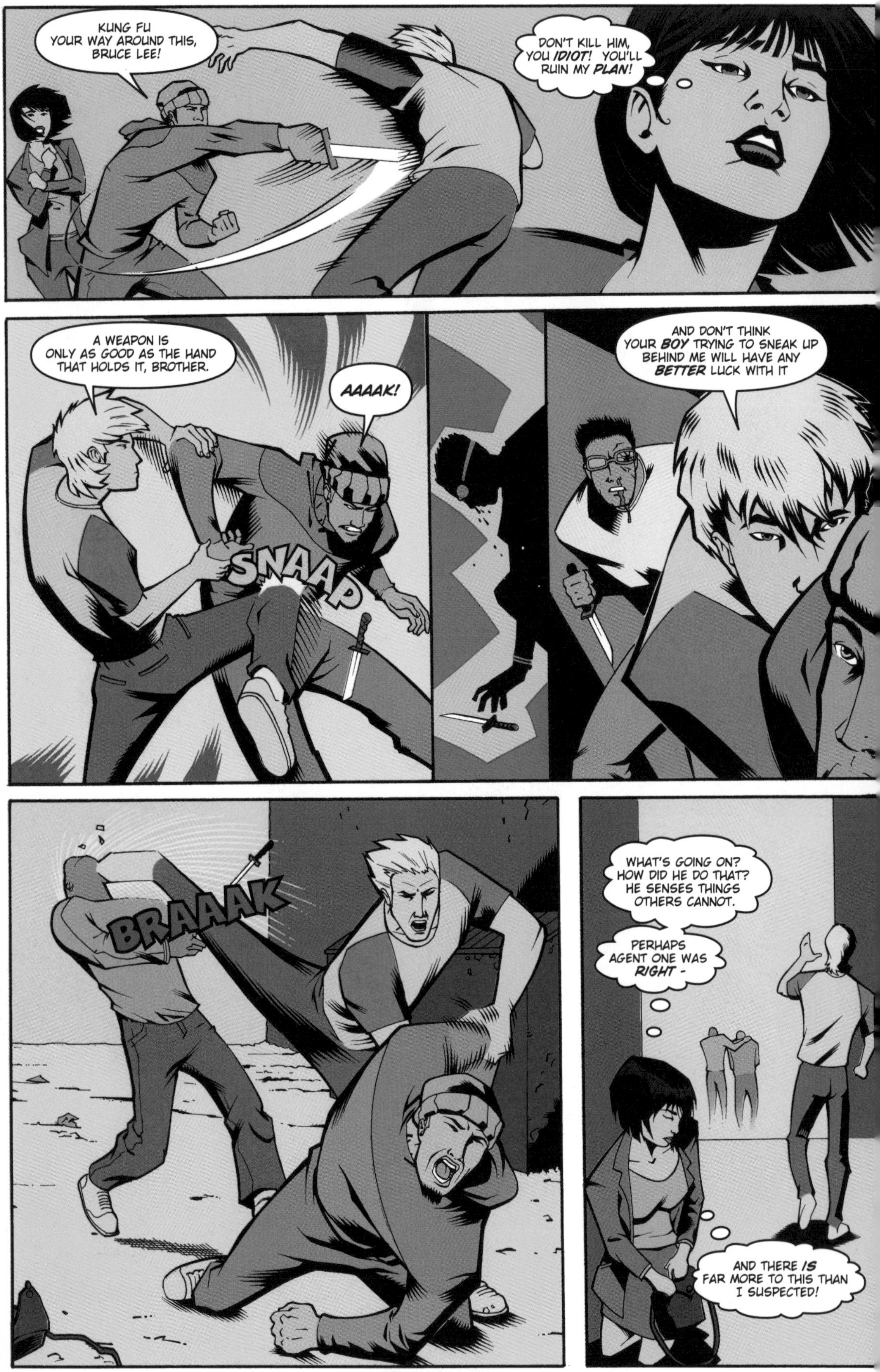
KUNG FU YOUR WAY AROUND THIS, BRUCE LEE!
DON'T KILL HIM, YOU IDIOT! YOU'LL RUIN MY PLAN!
A WEAPON IS ONLY AS GOOD AS THE HAND THAT HOLDS IT, BROTHER.
AAAAK!
SNAAP
AND DON'T THINK YOUR BOY TRYING TO SNEAK UP BEHIND ME WILL HAVE ANY BETTER LUCK WITH IT
BRAAAK
WHAT'S GOING ON? HOW DID HE DO THAT? HE SENSES THINGS OTHERS CANNOT.
PERHAPS AGENT ONE WAS RIGHT -
AND THERE IS FAR MORE TO THIS THAN I SUSPECTED!

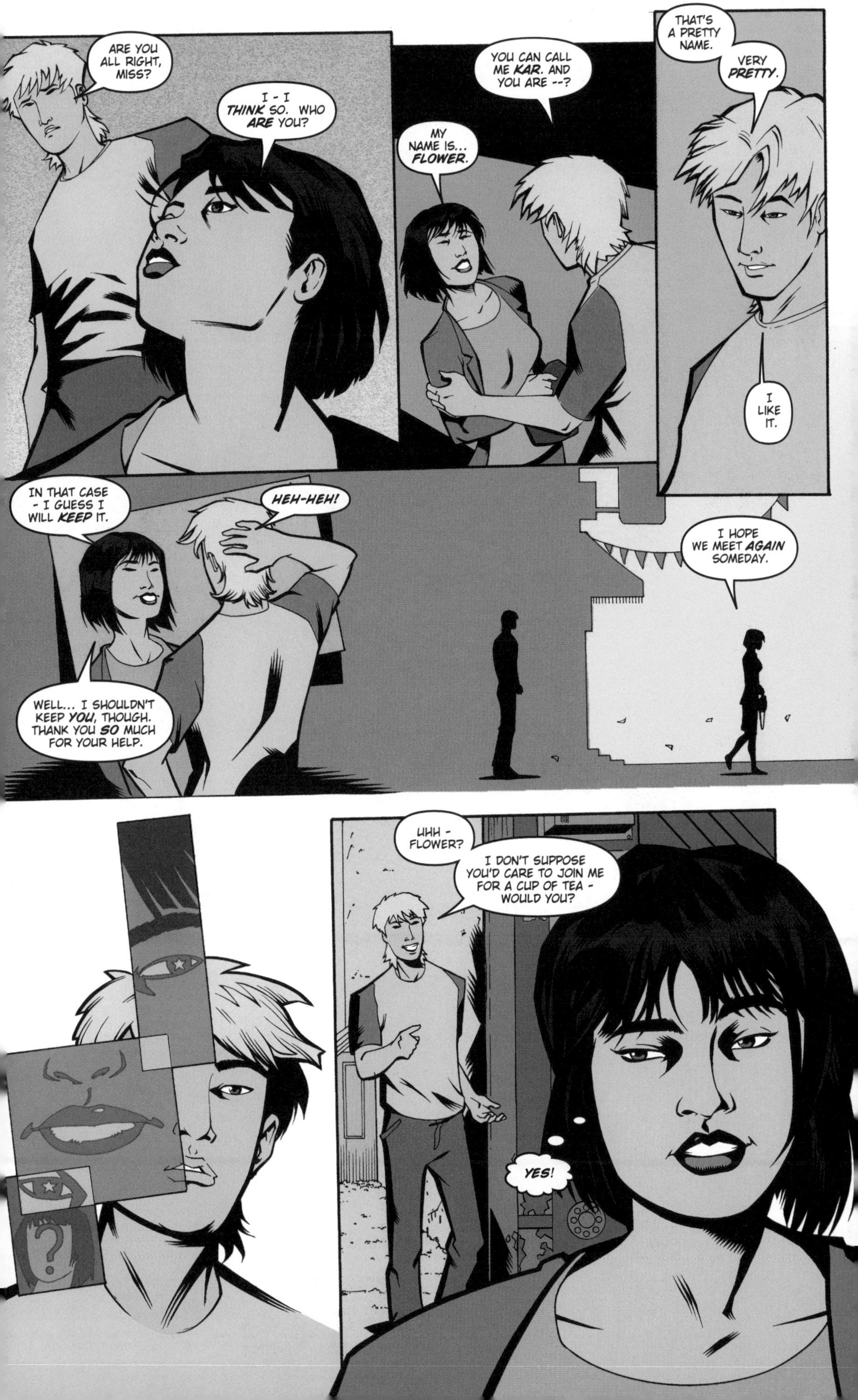
ARE YOU ALL RIGHT, MISS?
I - I THINK SO. WHO ARE YOU?
YOU CAN CALL ME KAR. AND YOU ARE --?
MY NAME IS... FLOWER.
THAT'S A PRETTY NAME.
VERY PRETTY.
I LIKE IT.
IN THAT CASE - I GUESS I WILL KEEP IT.
HEH-HEH!
WELL... I SHOULDN'T KEEP YOU, THOUGH. THANK YOU SO MUCH FOR YOUR HELP.
I HOPE WE MEET AGAIN SOMEDAY.
UHH - FLOWER?
I DON'T SUPPOSE YOU'D CARE TO JOIN ME FOR A CUP OF TEA - WOULD YOU?
YES!

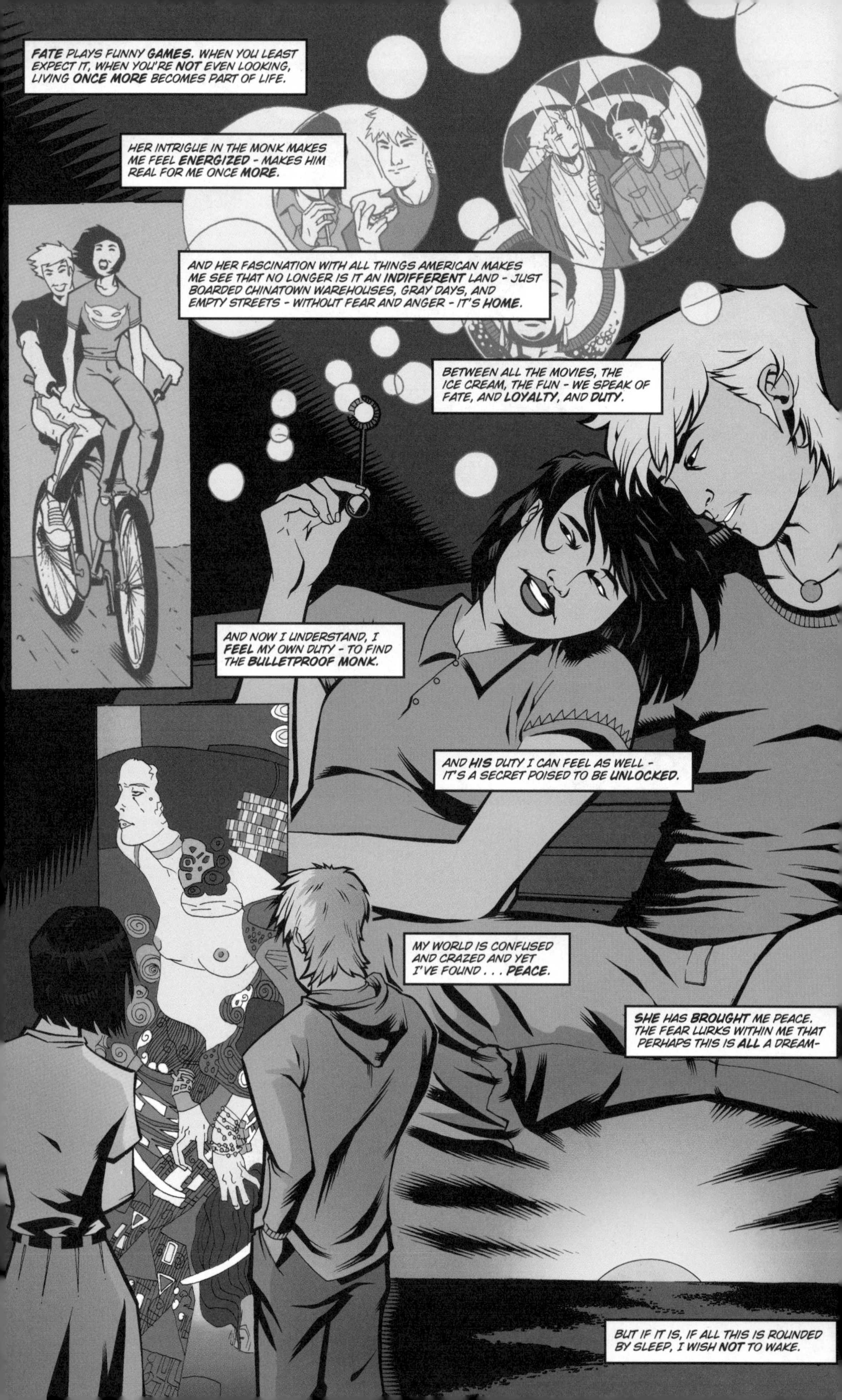
FATE PLAYS FUNNY GAMES. WHEN YOU LEAST EXPECT IT, WHEN YOU'RE NOT EVEN LOOKING, LIVING ONCE MORE BECOMES PART OF LIFE.
HER INTRIGUE IN THE MONK MAKES ME FEEL ENERGIZED - MAKES HIM REAL FOR ME ONCE MORE.
AND HER FASCINATION WITH ALL THINGS AMERICAN MAKES ME SEE THAT NO LONGER IS IT AN INDIFFERENT LAND - JUST BOARDED CHINATOWN WAREHOUSES, GRAY DAYS, AND EMPTY STREETS - WITHOUT FEAR AND ANGER - IT'S HOME.
BETWEEN ALL THE MOVIES, THE ICE CREAM, THE FUN - WE SPEAK OF FATE, AND LOYALTY, AND DUTY.
AND NOW I UNDERSTAND, I FEEL MY OWN DUTY - TO FIND THE BULLETPROOF MONK.
AND HIS DUTY I CAN FEEL AS WELL - IT'S A SECRET POISED TO BE UNLOCKED.
MY WORLD IS CONFUSED AND CRAZED AND YET I'VE FOUND . . . PEACE.
SHE HAS BROUGHT ME PEACE. THE FEAR LURKS WITHIN ME THAT PERHAPS THIS IS ALL A DREAM-
BUT IF IT IS, IF ALL THIS IS ROUNDED BY SLEEP, I WISH NOT TO WAKE.

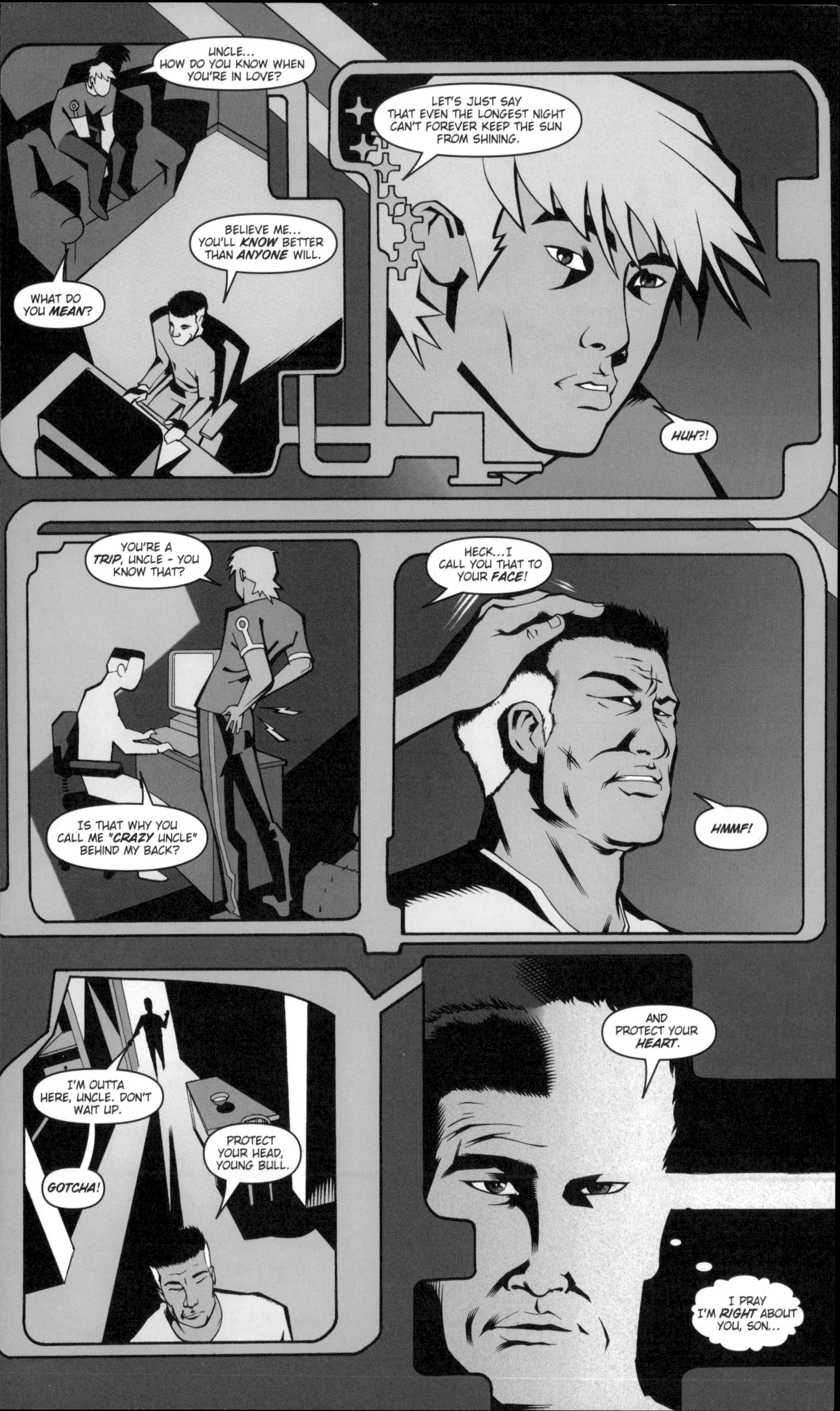
UNCLE... HOW DO YOU KNOW WHEN YOU'RE IN LOVE?
BELIEVE ME... YOU'LL **KNOW** BETTER THAN **ANYONE** WILL.
WHAT DO YOU **MEAN**?
LET'S JUST SAY THAT EVEN THE LONGEST NIGHT CAN'T FOREVER KEEP THE SUN FROM SHINING.
**HUH?!**
YOU'RE A **TRIP**, UNCLE - YOU KNOW THAT?
IS THAT WHY YOU CALL ME "**CRAZY** UNCLE" BEHIND MY BACK?
HECK...I CALL YOU THAT TO YOUR **FACE!**
**HMMF!**
I'M OUTTA HERE, UNCLE. DON'T WAIT UP.
PROTECT YOUR HEAD, YOUNG BULL.
**GOTCHA!**
AND PROTECT YOUR **HEART**.
I PRAY I'M **RIGHT** ABOUT YOU, SON...

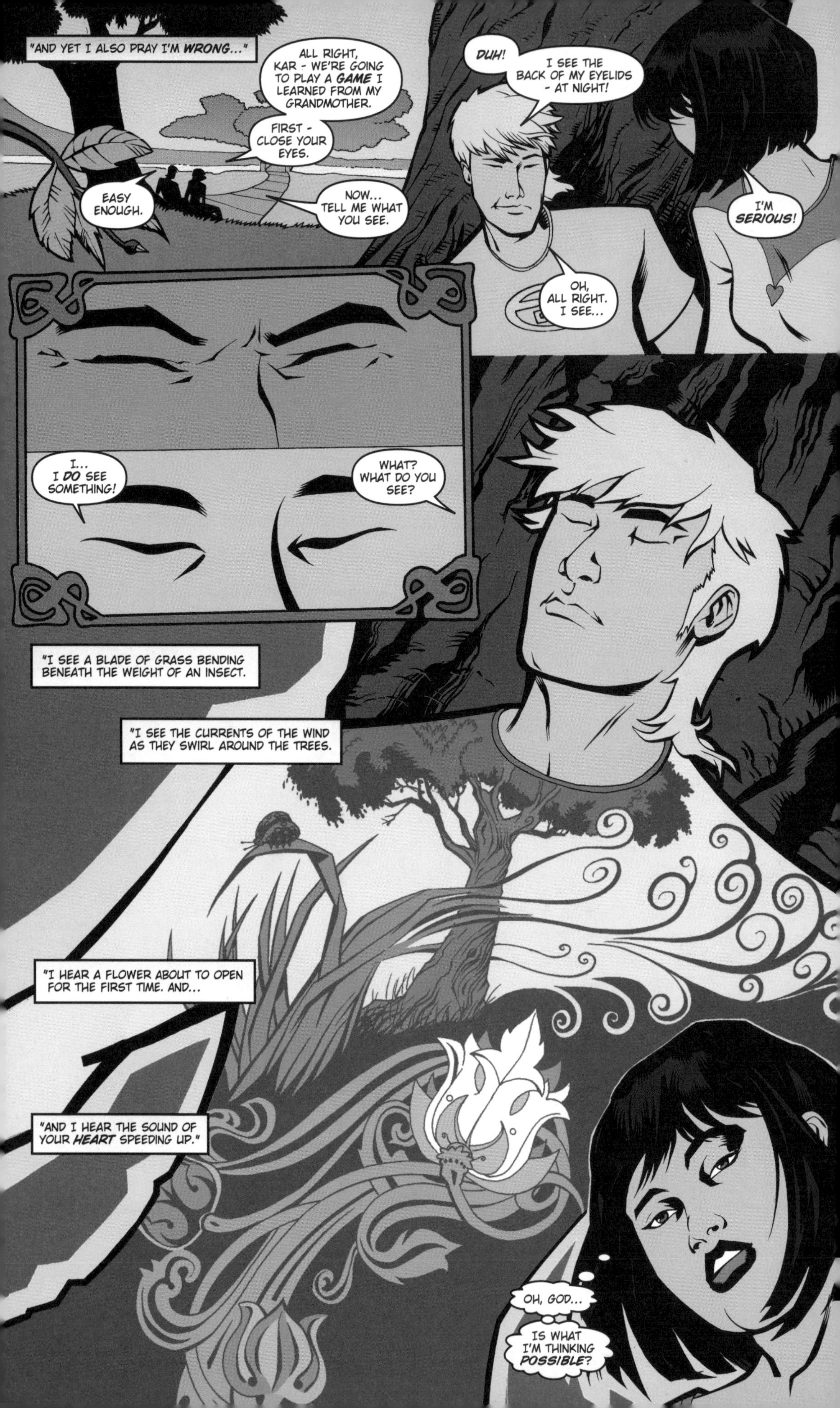
"AND YET I ALSO PRAY I'M WRONG..."
ALL RIGHT, KAR - WE'RE GOING TO PLAY A GAME I LEARNED FROM MY GRANDMOTHER.
FIRST - CLOSE YOUR EYES.
EASY ENOUGH.
NOW... TELL ME WHAT YOU SEE.
DUH!
I SEE THE BACK OF MY EYELIDS - AT NIGHT!
I'M SERIOUS!
OH, ALL RIGHT. I SEE...
I... I DO SEE SOMETHING!
WHAT? WHAT DO YOU SEE?
"I SEE A BLADE OF GRASS BENDING BENEATH THE WEIGHT OF AN INSECT.
"I SEE THE CURRENTS OF THE WIND AS THEY SWIRL AROUND THE TREES.
"I HEAR A FLOWER ABOUT TO OPEN FOR THE FIRST TIME. AND...
"AND I HEAR THE SOUND OF YOUR HEART SPEEDING UP."
OH, GOD...
IS WHAT I'M THINKING POSSIBLE?

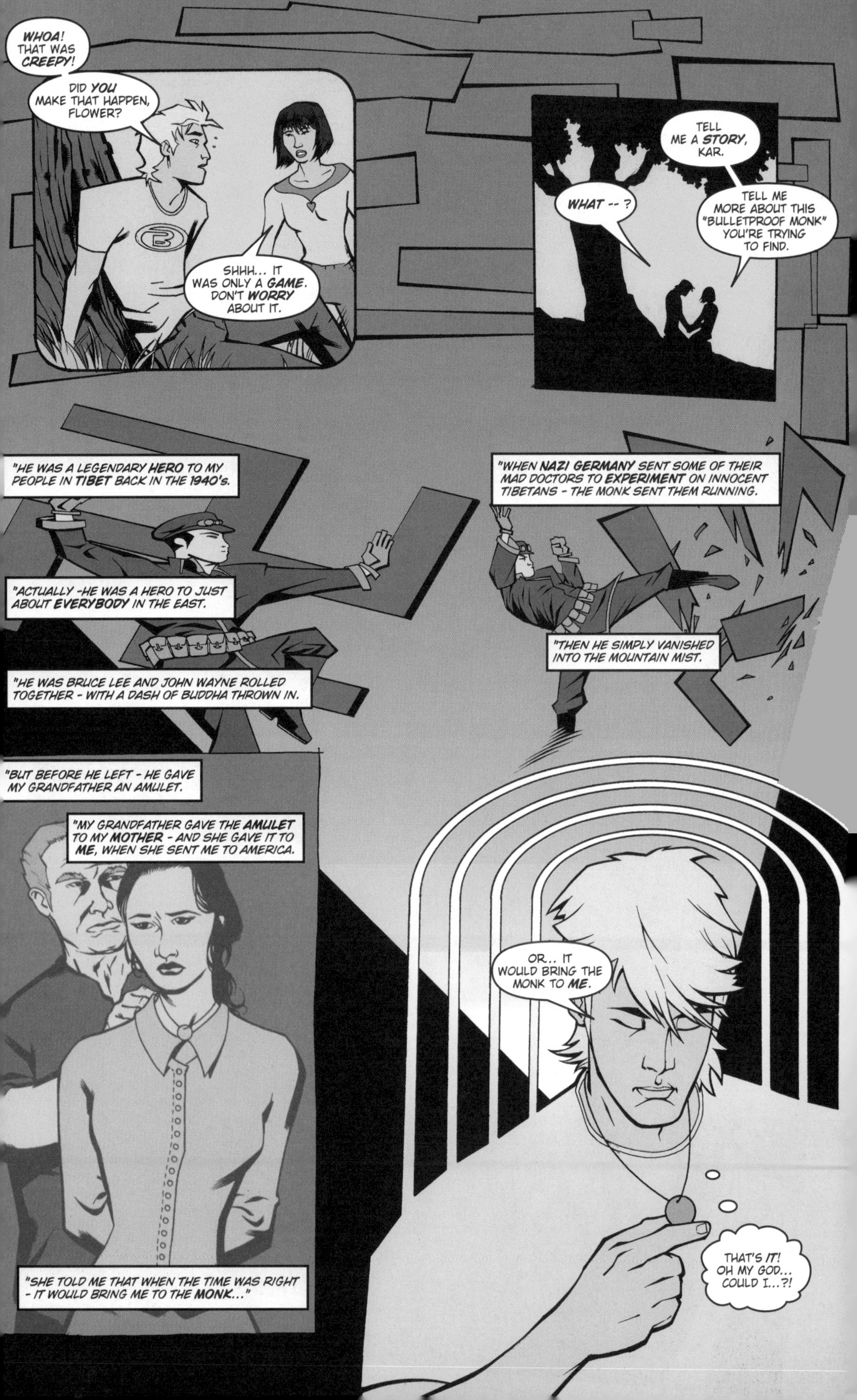
WHOA! THAT WAS CREEPY!
DID YOU MAKE THAT HAPPEN, FLOWER?
SHHH... IT WAS ONLY A GAME. DON'T WORRY ABOUT IT.
TELL ME A STORY, KAR.
WHAT -- ?
TELL ME MORE ABOUT THIS "BULLETPROOF MONK" YOU'RE TRYING TO FIND.
"HE WAS A LEGENDARY HERO TO MY PEOPLE IN TIBET BACK IN THE 1940's.
"ACTUALLY -HE WAS A HERO TO JUST ABOUT EVERYBODY IN THE EAST.
"HE WAS BRUCE LEE AND JOHN WAYNE ROLLED TOGETHER - WITH A DASH OF BUDDHA THROWN IN.
"WHEN NAZI GERMANY SENT SOME OF THEIR MAD DOCTORS TO EXPERIMENT ON INNOCENT TIBETANS - THE MONK SENT THEM RUNNING.
"THEN HE SIMPLY VANISHED INTO THE MOUNTAIN MIST.
"BUT BEFORE HE LEFT - HE GAVE MY GRANDFATHER AN AMULET.
"MY GRANDFATHER GAVE THE AMULET TO MY MOTHER - AND SHE GAVE IT TO ME, WHEN SHE SENT ME TO AMERICA.
"SHE TOLD ME THAT WHEN THE TIME WAS RIGHT - IT WOULD BRING ME TO THE MONK..."
OR.. IT WOULD BRING THE MONK TO ME.
THAT'S IT! OH MY GOD... COULD I...?!

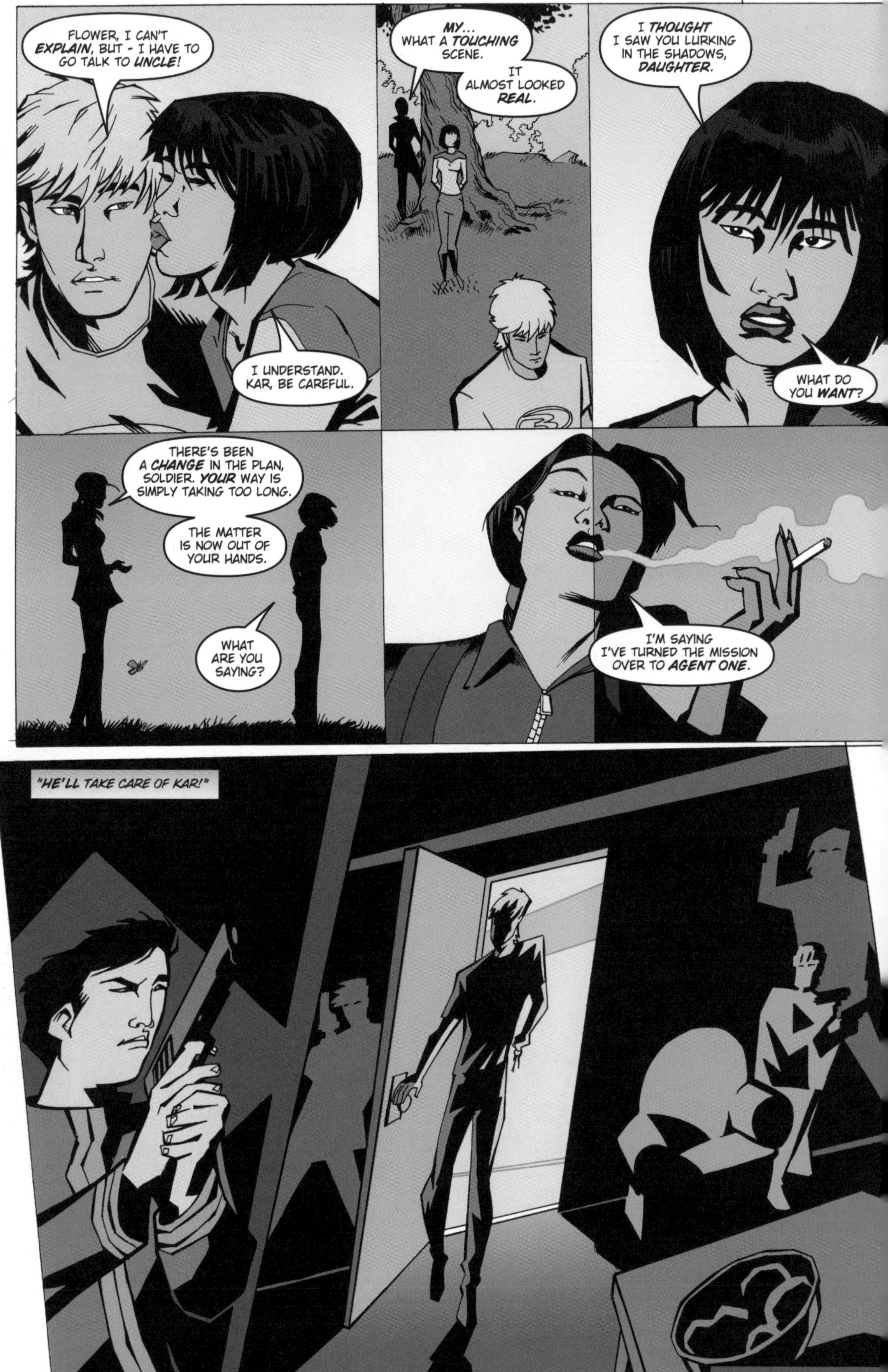
FLOWER, I CAN'T EXPLAIN, BUT - I HAVE TO GO TALK TO UNCLE!
I UNDERSTAND. KAR, BE CAREFUL.
MY... WHAT A TOUCHING SCENE.
IT ALMOST LOOKED REAL.
I THOUGHT I SAW YOU LURKING IN THE SHADOWS, DAUGHTER.
WHAT DO YOU WANT?
THERE'S BEEN A CHANGE IN THE PLAN, SOLDIER. YOUR WAY IS SIMPLY TAKING TOO LONG.
THE MATTER IS NOW OUT OF YOUR HANDS.
WHAT ARE YOU SAYING?
I'M SAYING I'VE TURNED THE MISSION OVER TO AGENT ONE.
"HE'LL TAKE CARE OF KAR!"
CONCLUDED NEXT ISSUE! -

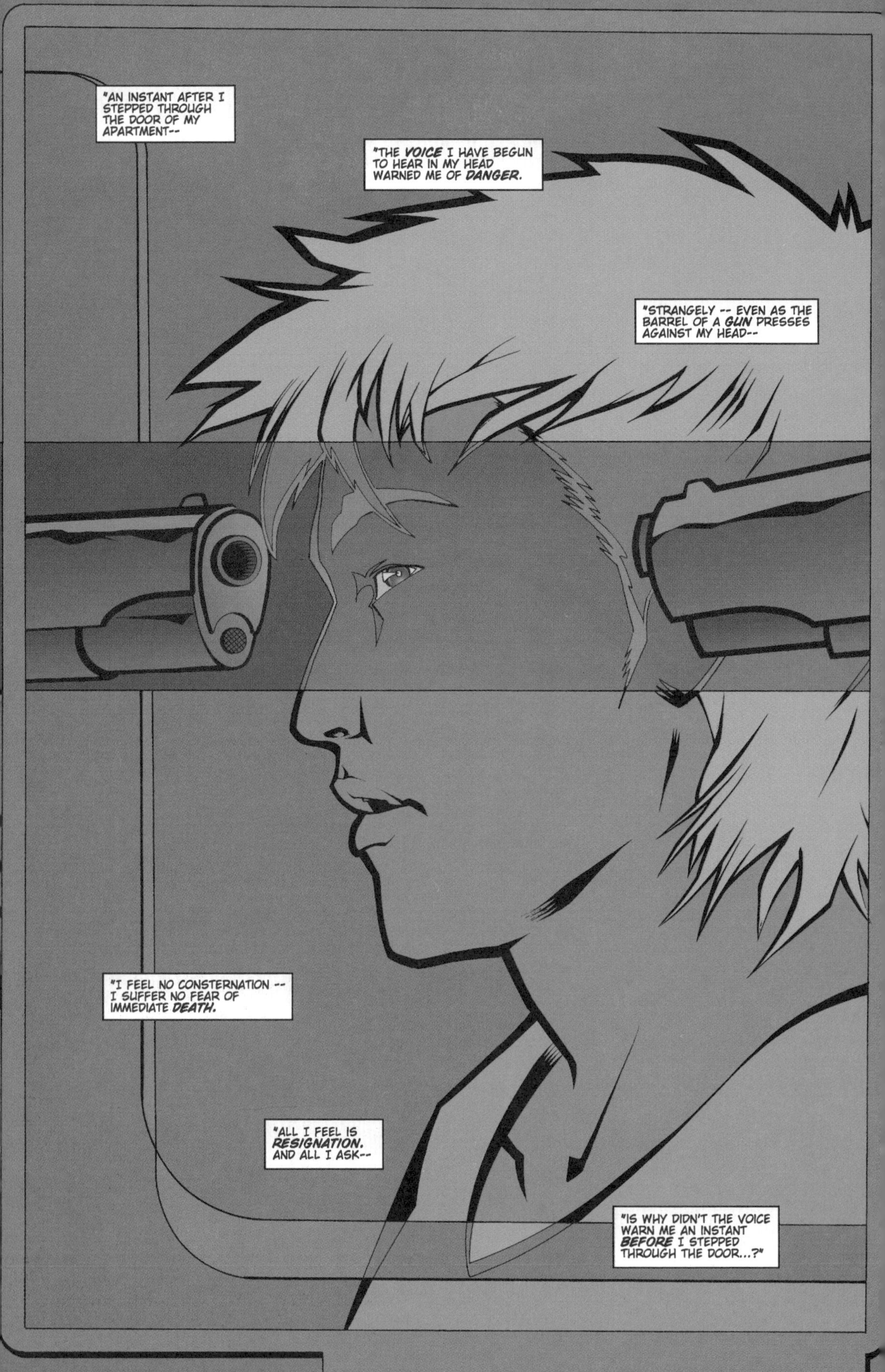
"AN INSTANT AFTER I STEPPED THROUGH THE DOOR OF MY APARTMENT--
"THE VOICE I HAVE BEGUN TO HEAR IN MY HEAD WARNED ME OF DANGER.
"STRANGELY -- EVEN AS THE BARREL OF A GUN PRESSES AGAINST MY HEAD--
"I FEEL NO CONSTERNATION -- I SUFFER NO FEAR OF IMMEDIATE DEATH.
"ALL I FEEL IS RESIGNATION. AND ALL I ASK--
"IS WHY DIDN'T THE VOICE WARN ME AN INSTANT BEFORE I STEPPED THROUGH THE DOOR...?"

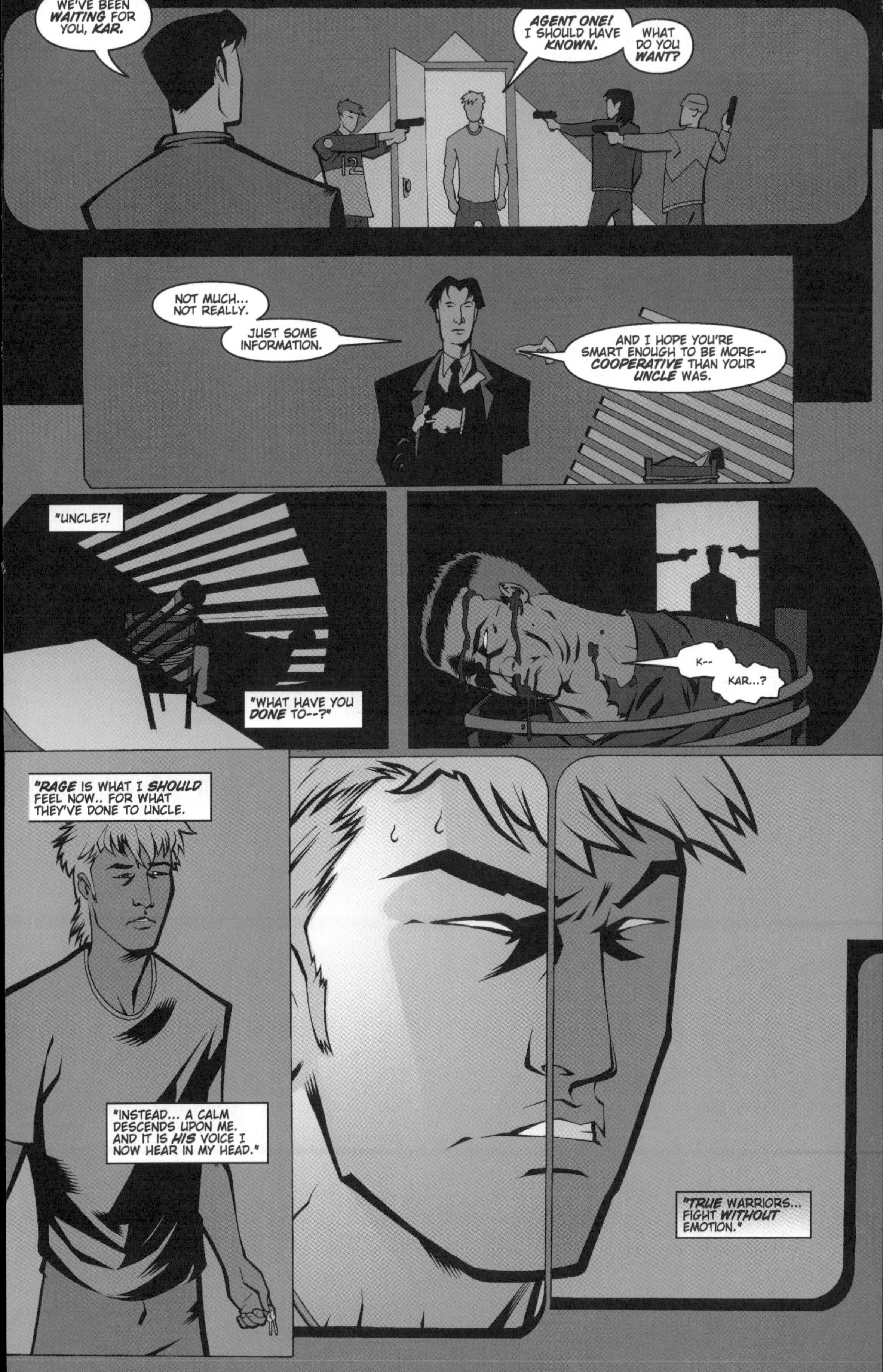
WE'VE BEEN WAITING FOR YOU, KAR.
AGENT ONE! I SHOULD HAVE KNOWN.
WHAT DO YOU WANT?
NOT MUCH... NOT REALLY.
JUST SOME INFORMATION.
AND I HOPE YOU'RE SMART ENOUGH TO BE MORE-- COOPERATIVE THAN YOUR UNCLE WAS.
"UNCLE?!
"WHAT HAVE YOU DONE TO--?"
K--
KAR...?
"RAGE IS WHAT I SHOULD FEEL NOW.. FOR WHAT THEY'VE DONE TO UNCLE.
"INSTEAD... A CALM DESCENDS UPON ME. AND IT IS HIS VOICE I NOW HEAR IN MY HEAD."
"TRUE WARRIORS... FIGHT WITHOUT EMOTION."

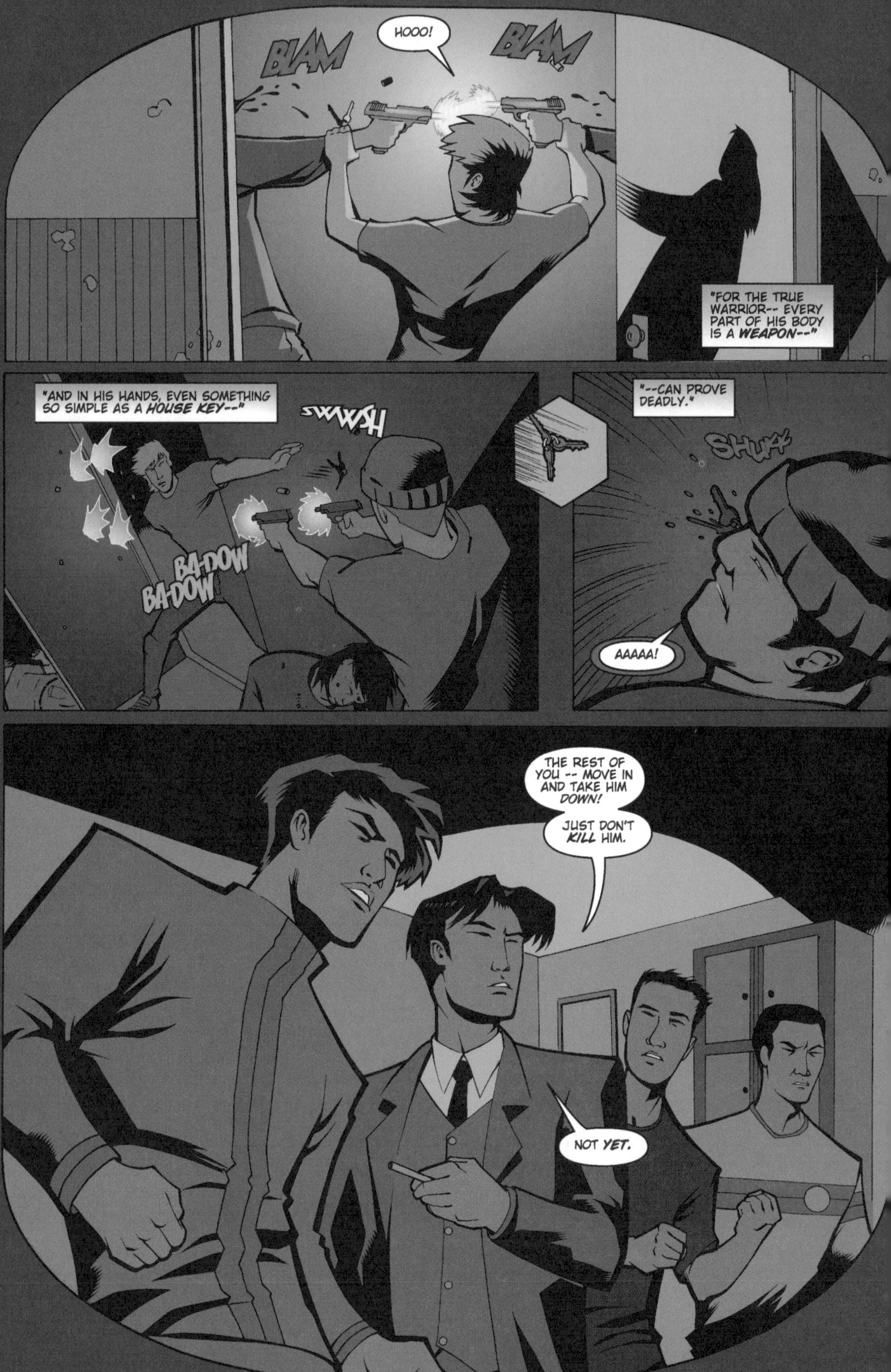
BLAM
HOOO!
BLAM
"FOR THE TRUE WARRIOR-- EVERY PART OF HIS BODY IS A WEAPON--"
"AND IN HIS HANDS, EVEN SOMETHING SO SIMPLE AS A HOUSE KEY--"
SWAWSH
BA-DOW
BA-DOW
"--CAN PROVE DEADLY."
SHUK
AAAAA!
THE REST OF YOU -- MOVE IN AND TAKE HIM DOWN!
JUST DON'T KILL HIM.
NOT YET.

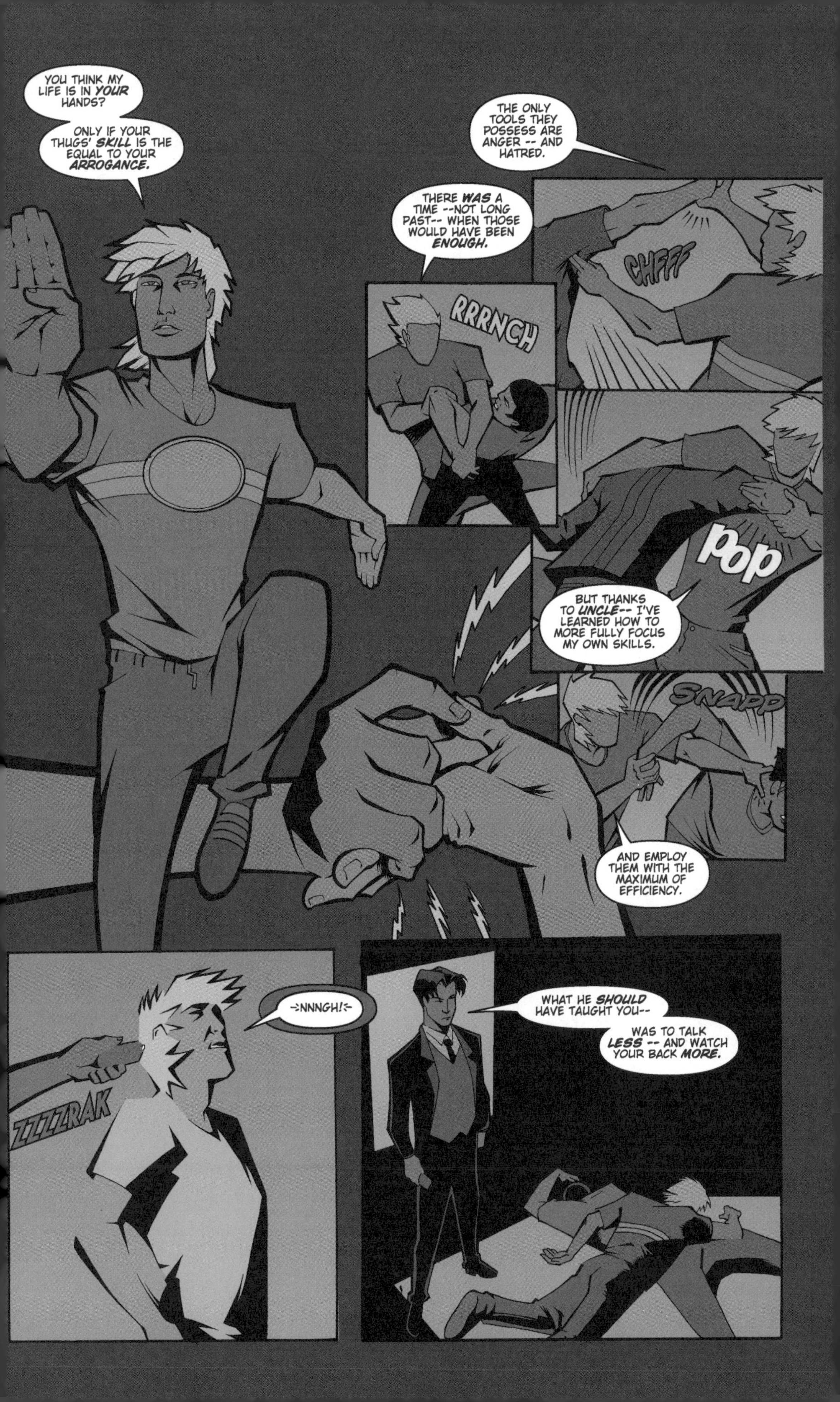
YOU THINK MY LIFE IS IN YOUR HANDS?
ONLY IF YOUR THUGS' SKILL IS THE EQUAL TO YOUR ARROGANCE.
THE ONLY TOOLS THEY POSSESS ARE ANGER -- AND HATRED.
THERE WAS A TIME --NOT LONG PAST-- WHEN THOSE WOULD HAVE BEEN ENOUGH.
CHFFF
RRRNCH
POP
BUT THANKS TO UNCLE-- I'VE LEARNED HOW TO MORE FULLY FOCUS MY OWN SKILLS.
SNAPP
AND EMPLOY THEM WITH THE MAXIMUM OF EFFICIENCY.
ZZZZRAK
NNNGH!
WHAT HE SHOULD HAVE TAUGHT YOU--
WAS TO TALK LESS -- AND WATCH YOUR BACK MORE.

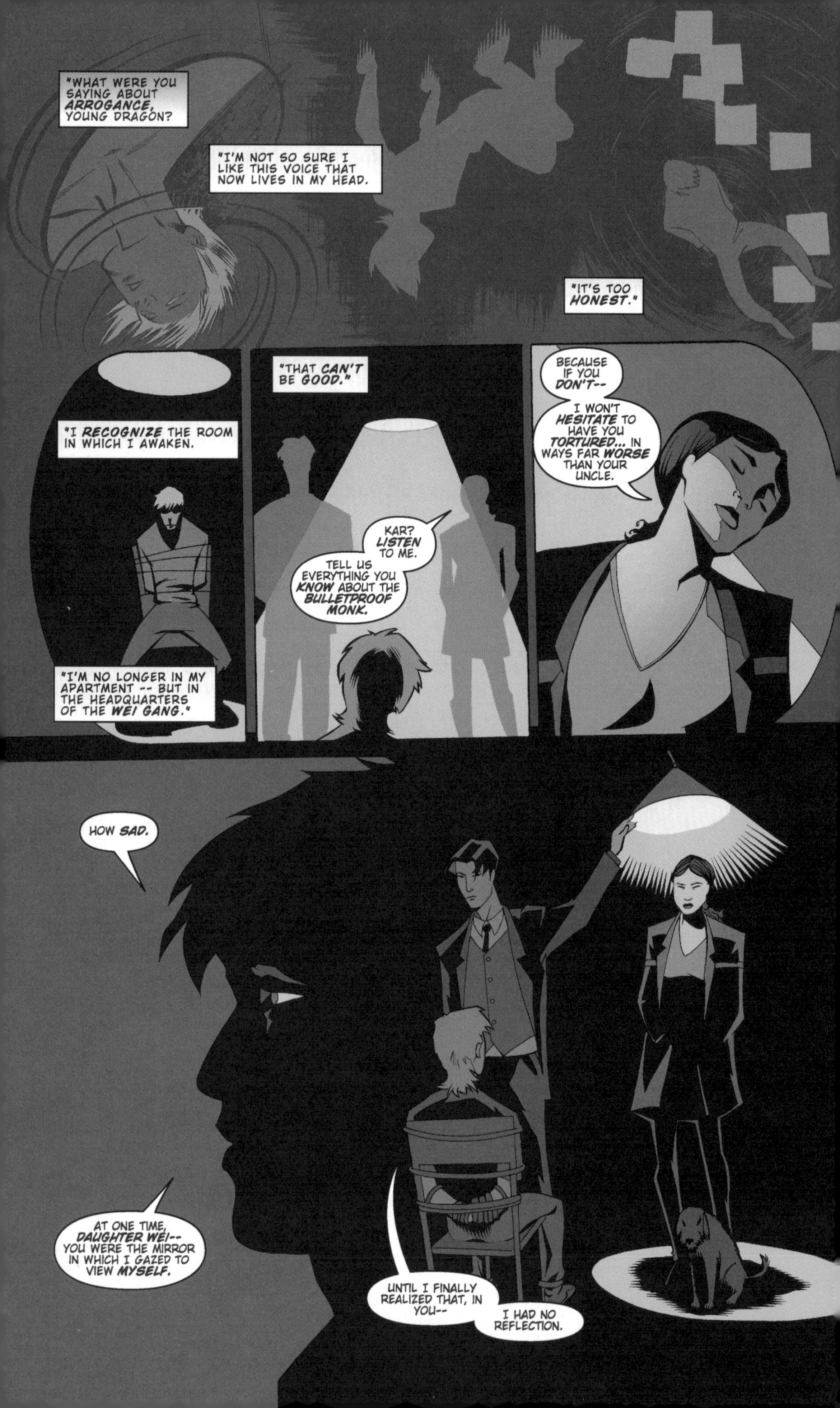
"WHAT WERE YOU SAYING ABOUT ARROGANCE, YOUNG DRAGON?
"I'M NOT SO SURE I LIKE THIS VOICE THAT NOW LIVES IN MY HEAD.
"IT'S TOO HONEST."
"I RECOGNIZE THE ROOM IN WHICH I AWAKEN.
"I'M NO LONGER IN MY APARTMENT -- BUT IN THE HEADQUARTERS OF THE WEI GANG."
"THAT CAN'T BE GOOD."
KAR? LISTEN TO ME.
TELL US EVERYTHING YOU KNOW ABOUT THE BULLETPROOF MONK.
BECAUSE IF YOU DON'T--
I WON'T HESITATE TO HAVE YOU TORTURED... IN WAYS FAR WORSE THAN YOUR UNCLE.
HOW SAD.
AT ONE TIME, DAUGHTER WEI-- YOU WERE THE MIRROR IN WHICH I GAZED TO VIEW MYSELF.
UNTIL I FINALLY REALIZED THAT, IN YOU--
I HAD NO REFLECTION.

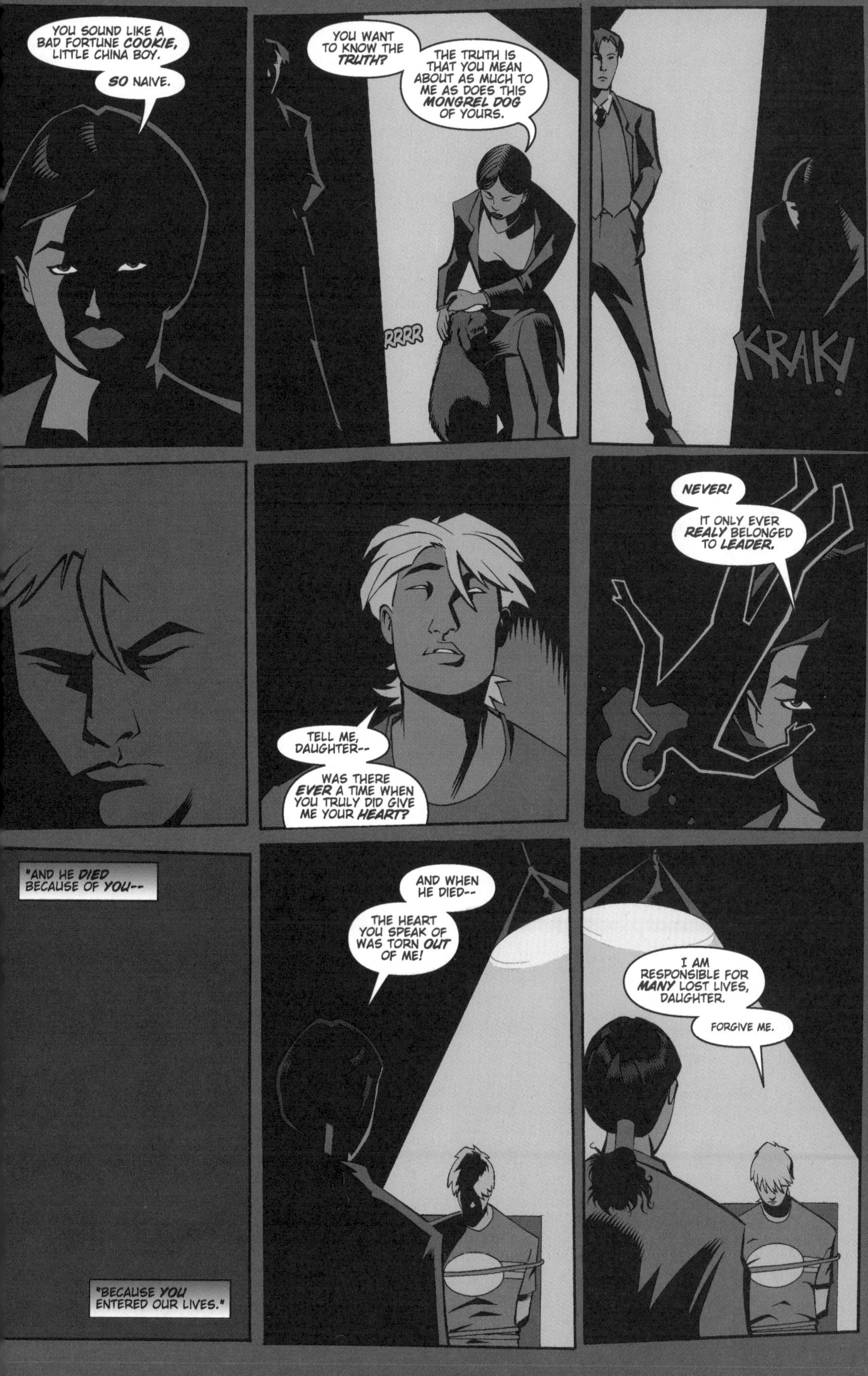
YOU SOUND LIKE A BAD FORTUNE COOKIE, LITTLE CHINA BOY.
SO NAIVE.
YOU WANT TO KNOW THE TRUTH?
THE TRUTH IS THAT YOU MEAN ABOUT AS MUCH TO ME AS DOES THIS MONGREL DOG OF YOURS.
RRRR
KRAK!
TELL ME, DAUGHTER--
WAS THERE EVER A TIME WHEN YOU TRULY DID GIVE ME YOUR HEART?
NEVER!
IT ONLY EVER REALY BELONGED TO LEADER.
"AND HE DIED BECAUSE OF YOU--
"BECAUSE YOU ENTERED OUR LIVES."
AND WHEN HE DIED--
THE HEART YOU SPEAK OF WAS TORN OUT OF ME!
I AM RESPONSIBLE FOR MANY LOST LIVES, DAUGHTER.
FORGIVE ME.

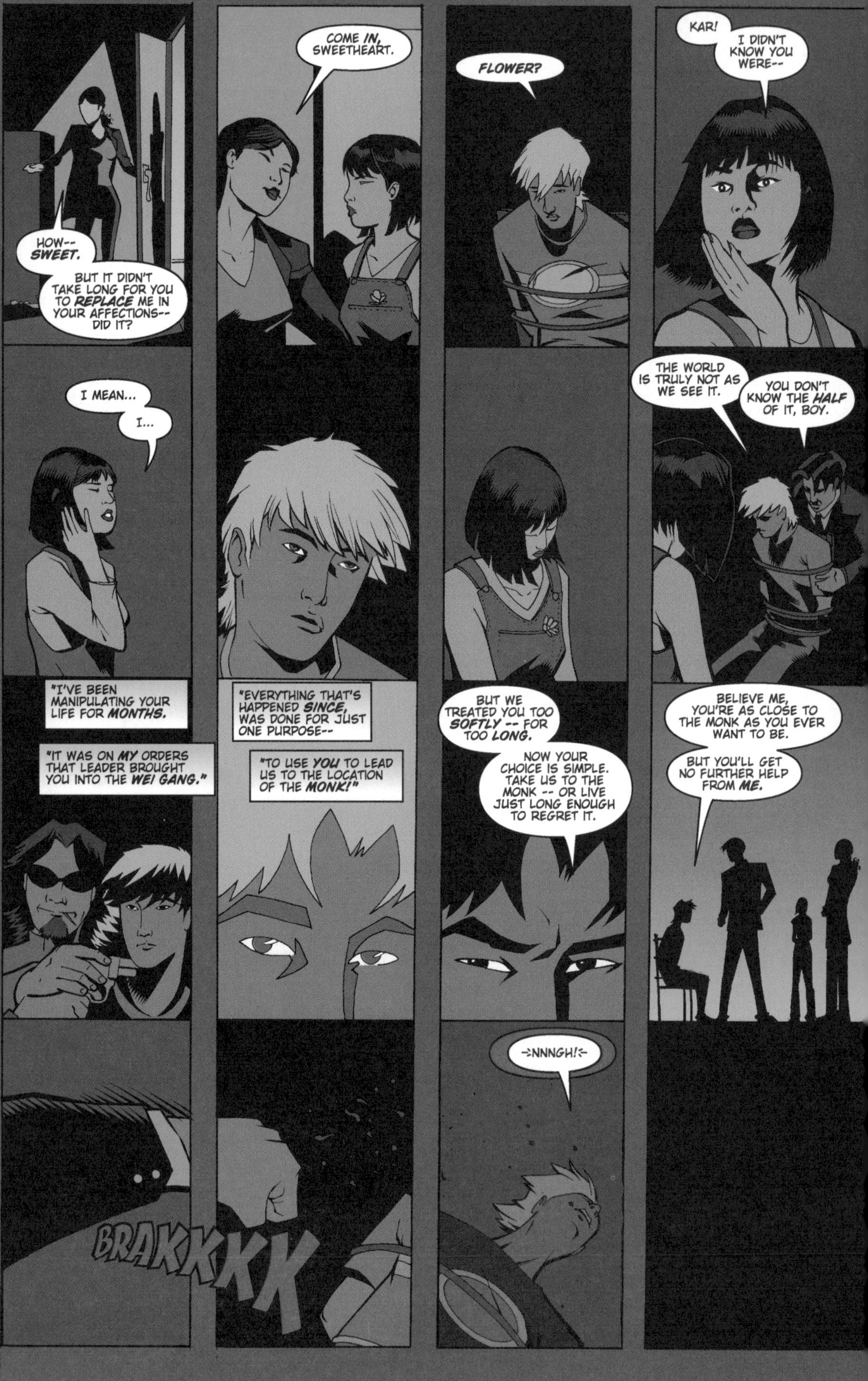
HOW-- SWEET.
BUT IT DIDN'T TAKE LONG FOR YOU TO REPLACE ME IN YOUR AFFECTIONS-- DID IT?
COME IN, SWEETHEART.
FLOWER?
KAR!
I DIDN'T KNOW YOU WERE--
I MEAN...
I...
THE WORLD IS TRULY NOT AS WE SEE IT.
YOU DON'T KNOW THE HALF OF IT, BOY.
"I'VE BEEN MANIPULATING YOUR LIFE FOR MONTHS.
"IT WAS ON MY ORDERS THAT LEADER BROUGHT YOU INTO THE WEI GANG."
"EVERYTHING THAT'S HAPPENED SINCE, WAS DONE FOR JUST ONE PURPOSE--
"TO USE YOU TO LEAD US TO THE LOCATION OF THE MONK!"
BUT WE TREATED YOU TOO SOFTLY -- FOR TOO LONG.
NOW YOUR CHOICE IS SIMPLE. TAKE US TO THE MONK -- OR LIVE JUST LONG ENOUGH TO REGRET IT.
BELIEVE ME, YOU'RE AS CLOSE TO THE MONK AS YOU EVER WANT TO BE.
BUT YOU'LL GET NO FURTHER HELP FROM ME.
BRAKKKK
-NNNGH!-

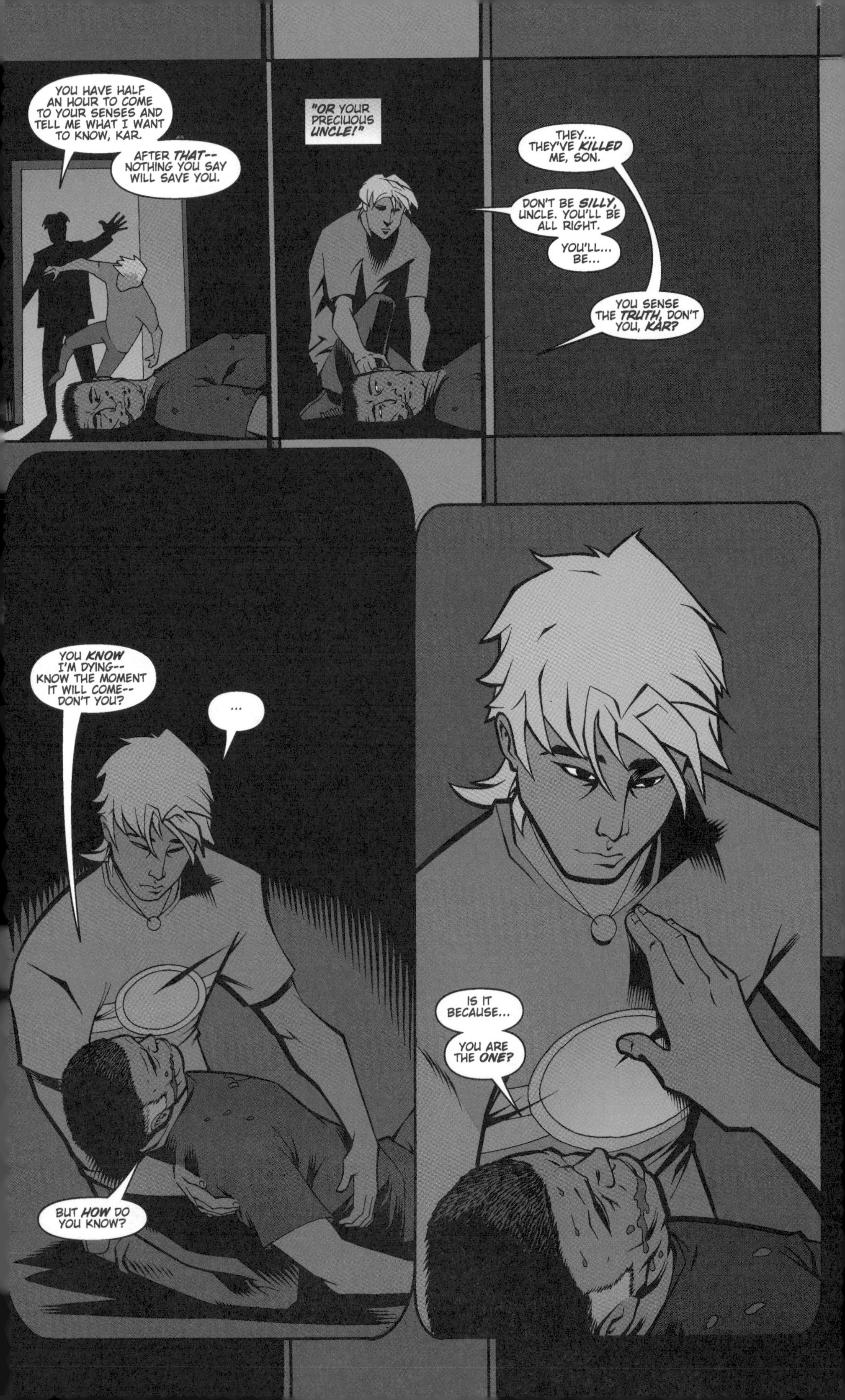
YOU HAVE HALF AN HOUR TO COME TO YOUR SENSES AND TELL ME WHAT I WANT TO KNOW, KAR.
AFTER THAT-- NOTHING YOU SAY WILL SAVE YOU.
"OR YOUR PRECIUOUS UNCLE!"
THEY... THEY'VE KILLED ME, SON.
DON'T BE SILLY, UNCLE. YOU'LL BE ALL RIGHT.
YOU'LL... BE...
YOU SENSE THE TRUTH, DON'T YOU, KAR?
YOU KNOW I'M DYING-- KNOW THE MOMENT IT WILL COME-- DON'T YOU?
...
BUT HOW DO YOU KNOW?
IS IT BECAUSE...
YOU ARE THE ONE?

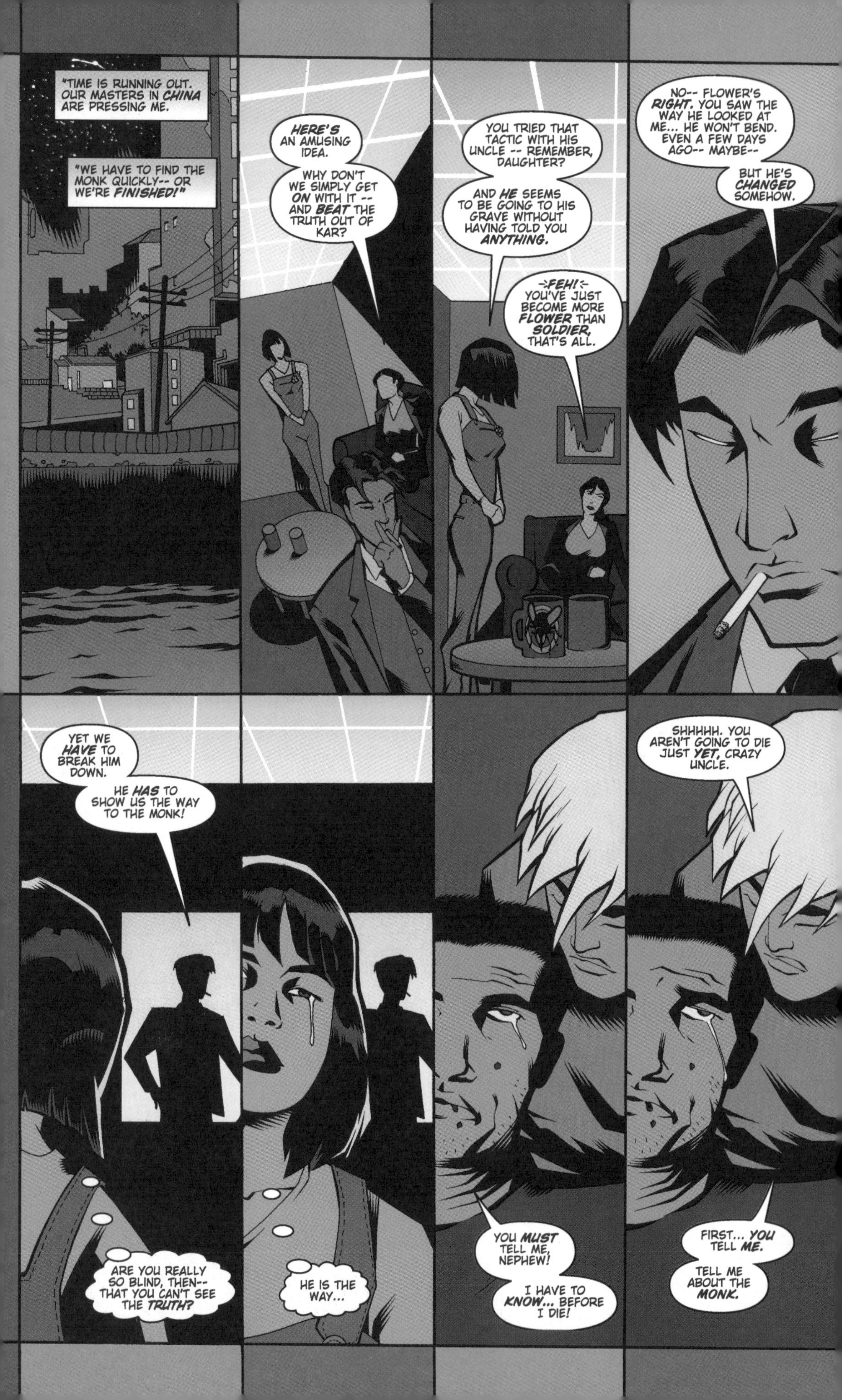
"TIME IS RUNNING OUT. OUR MASTERS IN CHINA ARE PRESSING ME.
"WE HAVE TO FIND THE MONK QUICKLY-- OR WE'RE FINISHED!"
HERE'S AN AMUSING IDEA.
WHY DON'T WE SIMPLY GET ON WITH IT -- AND BEAT THE TRUTH OUT OF KAR?
YOU TRIED THAT TACTIC WITH HIS UNCLE -- REMEMBER, DAUGHTER?
AND HE SEEMS TO BE GOING TO HIS GRAVE WITHOUT HAVING TOLD YOU ANYTHING.
FEH! YOU'VE JUST BECOME MORE FLOWER THAN SOLDIER, THAT'S ALL.
NO-- FLOWER'S RIGHT. YOU SAW THE WAY HE LOOKED AT ME... HE WON'T BEND. EVEN A FEW DAYS AGO-- MAYBE--
BUT HE'S CHANGED SOMEHOW.
YET WE HAVE TO BREAK HIM DOWN.
HE HAS TO SHOW US THE WAY TO THE MONK!
ARE YOU REALLY SO BLIND, THEN-- THAT YOU CAN'T SEE THE TRUTH?
HE IS THE WAY...
YOU MUST TELL ME, NEPHEW!
I HAVE TO KNOW... BEFORE I DIE!
SHHHHH. YOU AREN'T GOING TO DIE JUST YET, CRAZY UNCLE.
FIRST... YOU TELL ME.
TELL ME ABOUT THE MONK.

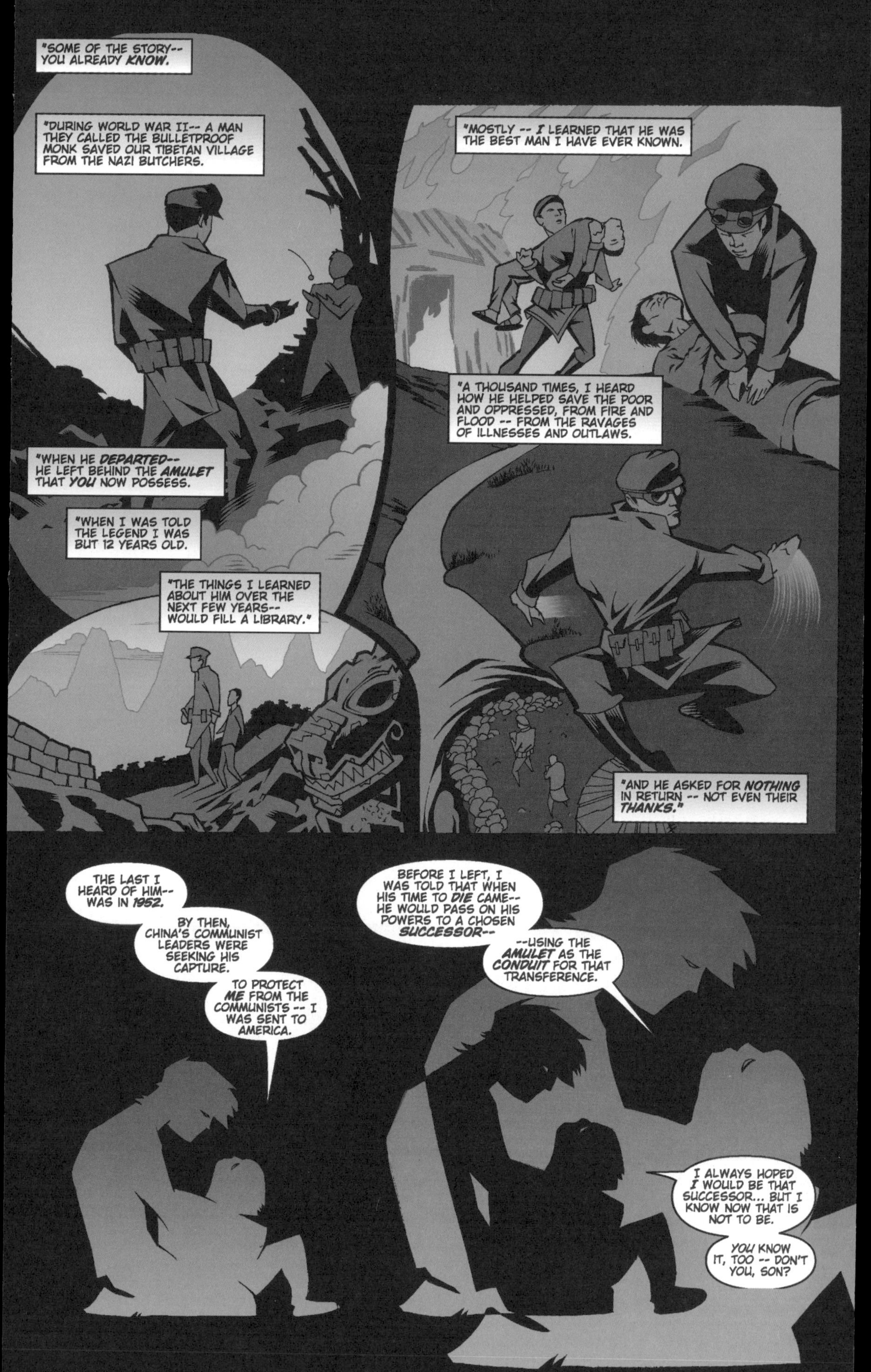
"SOME OF THE STORY-- YOU ALREADY KNOW.
"DURING WORLD WAR II-- A MAN THEY CALLED THE BULLETPROOF MONK SAVED OUR TIBETAN VILLAGE FROM THE NAZI BUTCHERS.
"WHEN HE DEPARTED-- HE LEFT BEHIND THE AMULET THAT YOU NOW POSSESS.
"WHEN I WAS TOLD THE LEGEND I WAS BUT 12 YEARS OLD.
"THE THINGS I LEARNED ABOUT HIM OVER THE NEXT FEW YEARS-- WOULD FILL A LIBRARY."
"MOSTLY -- I LEARNED THAT HE WAS THE BEST MAN I HAVE EVER KNOWN.
"A THOUSAND TIMES, I HEARD HOW HE HELPED SAVE THE POOR AND OPPRESSED, FROM FIRE AND FLOOD -- FROM THE RAVAGES OF ILLNESSES AND OUTLAWS.
"AND HE ASKED FOR NOTHING IN RETURN -- NOT EVEN THEIR THANKS."
THE LAST I HEARD OF HIM-- WAS IN 1952.
BY THEN, CHINA'S COMMUNIST LEADERS WERE SEEKING HIS CAPTURE.
TO PROTECT ME FROM THE COMMUNISTS -- I WAS SENT TO AMERICA.
BEFORE I LEFT, I WAS TOLD THAT WHEN HIS TIME TO DIE CAME-- HE WOULD PASS ON HIS POWERS TO A CHOSEN SUCCESSOR--
--USING THE AMULET AS THE CONDUIT FOR THAT TRANSFERENCE.
I ALWAYS HOPED I WOULD BE THAT SUCCESSOR... BUT I KNOW NOW THAT IS NOT TO BE.
YOU KNOW IT, TOO -- DON'T YOU, SON?

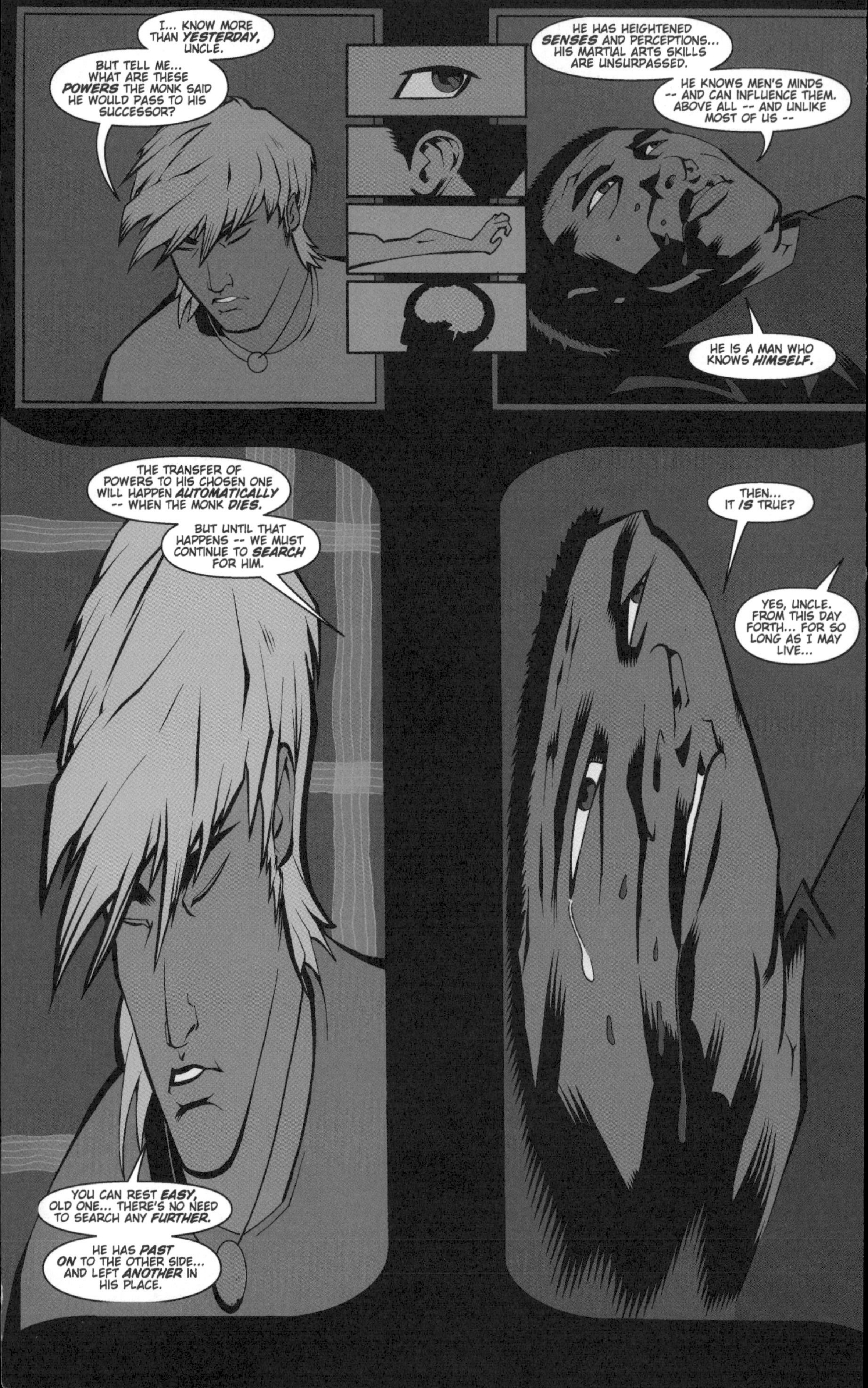

I... KNOW MORE THAN YESTERDAY, UNCLE.
BUT TELL ME... WHAT ARE THESE POWERS THE MONK SAID HE WOULD PASS TO HIS SUCCESSOR?
HE HAS HEIGHTENED SENSES AND PERCEPTIONS... HIS MARTIAL ARTS SKILLS ARE UNSURPASSED.
HE KNOWS MEN'S MINDS -- AND CAN INFLUENCE THEM. ABOVE ALL -- AND UNLIKE MOST OF US --
HE IS A MAN WHO KNOWS HIMSELF.
THE TRANSFER OF POWERS TO HIS CHOSEN ONE WILL HAPPEN AUTOMATICALLY -- WHEN THE MONK DIES.
BUT UNTIL THAT HAPPENS -- WE MUST CONTINUE TO SEARCH FOR HIM.
YOU CAN REST EASY, OLD ONE... THERE'S NO NEED TO SEARCH ANY FURTHER.
HE HAS PAST ON TO THE OTHER SIDE... AND LEFT ANOTHER IN HIS PLACE.
THEN... IT IS TRUE?
YES, UNCLE. FROM THIS DAY FORTH... FOR SO LONG AS I MAY LIVE...

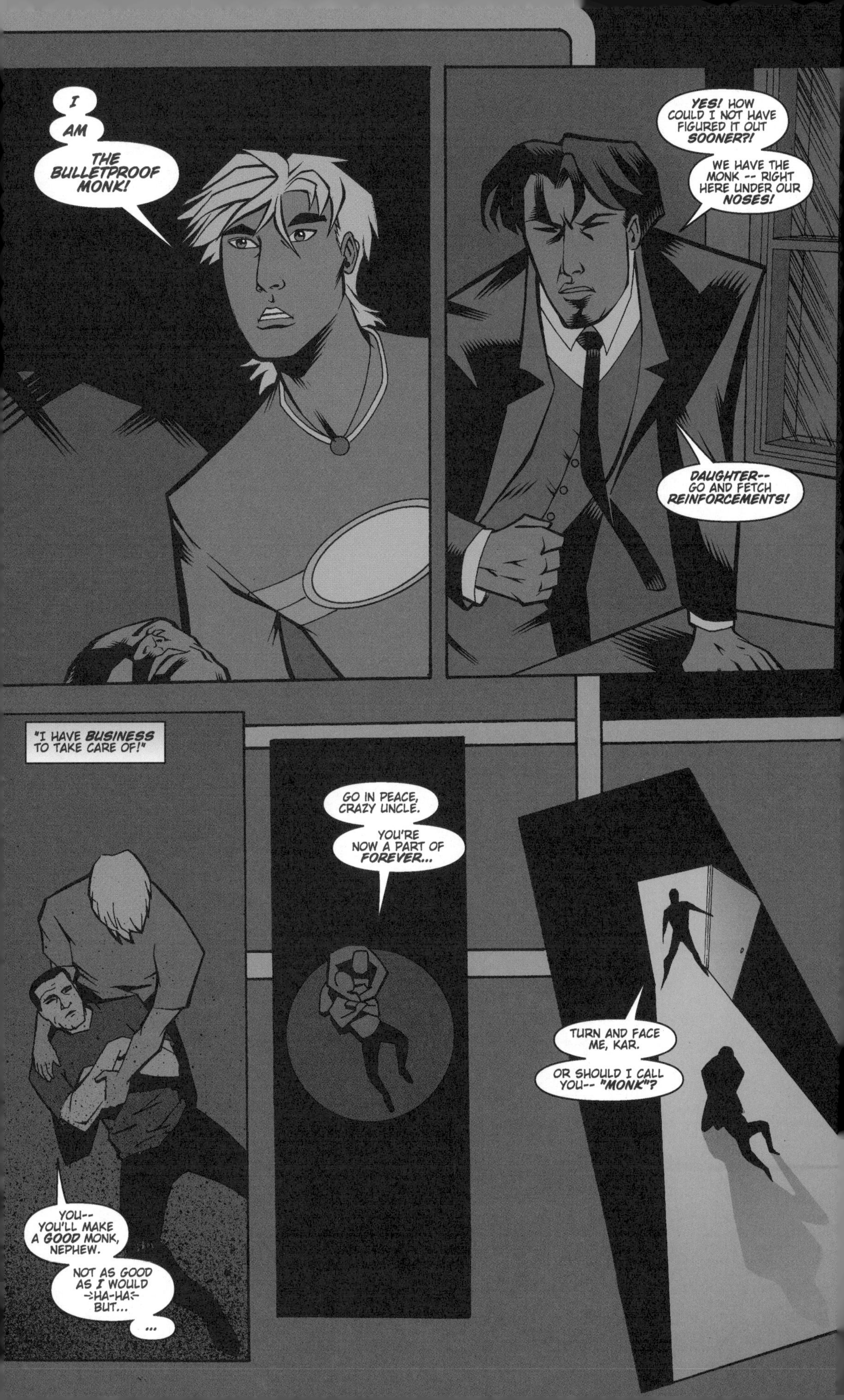
I
AM
THE BULLETPROOF MONK!
YES! HOW COULD I NOT HAVE FIGURED IT OUT SOONER?!
WE HAVE THE MONK -- RIGHT HERE UNDER OUR NOSES!
DAUGHTER-- GO AND FETCH REINFORCEMENTS!
"I HAVE BUSINESS TO TAKE CARE OF!"
YOU-- YOU'LL MAKE A GOOD MONK, NEPHEW.
NOT AS GOOD AS I WOULD -HA-HA- BUT...
...
GO IN PEACE, CRAZY UNCLE.
YOU'RE NOW A PART OF FOREVER...
TURN AND FACE ME, KAR.
OR SHOULD I CALL YOU-- "MONK"?

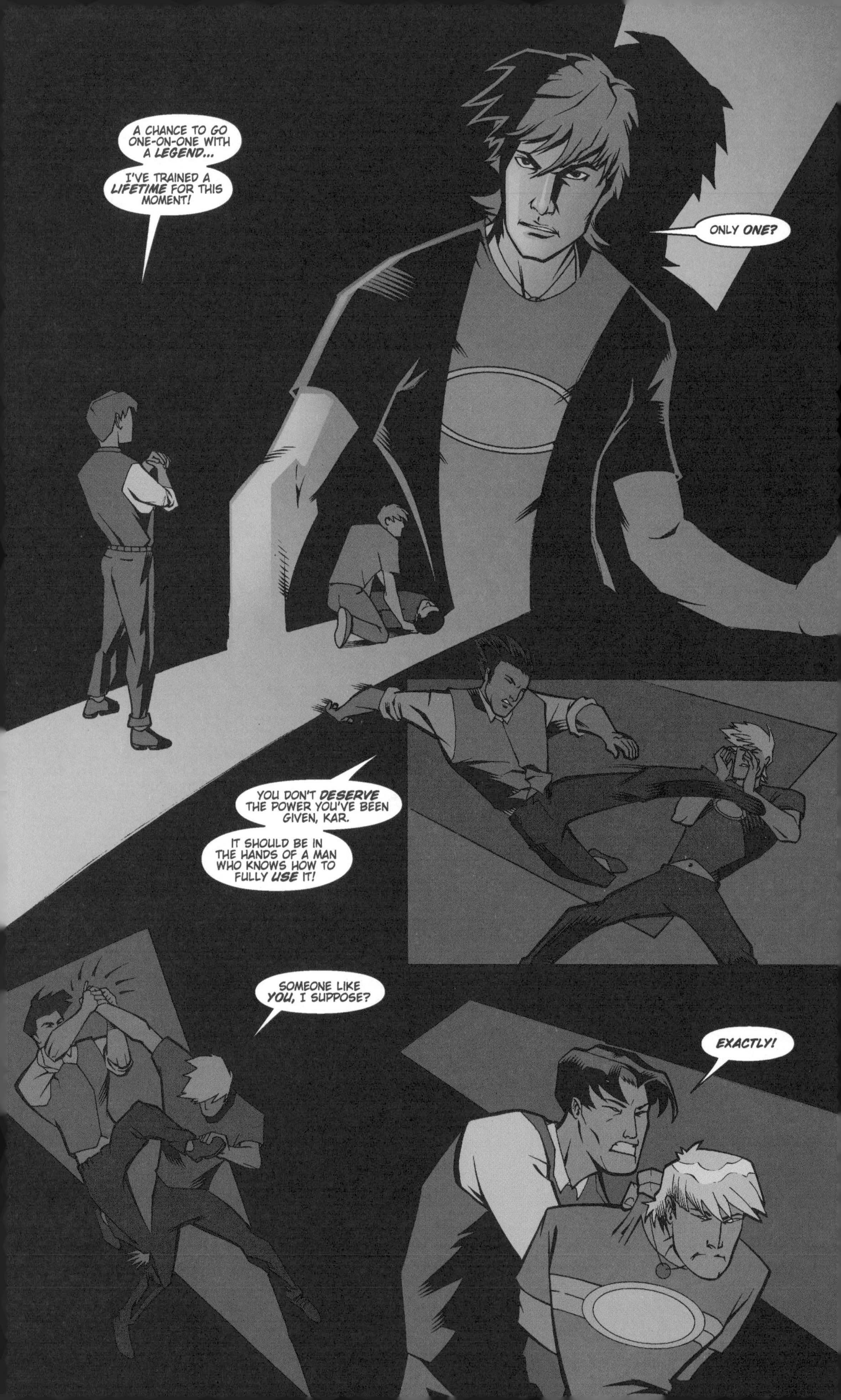

A CHANCE TO GO ONE-ON-ONE WITH A LEGENDS...
I'VE TRAINED A LIFETIME FOR THIS MOMENT!
ONLY ONE?
YOU DON'T DESERVE THE POWER YOU'VE BEEN GIVEN, KAR.
IT SHOULD BE IN THE HANDS OF A MAN WHO KNOWS HOW TO FULLY USE IT!
SOMEONE LIKE YOU, I SUPPOSE?
EXACTLY!

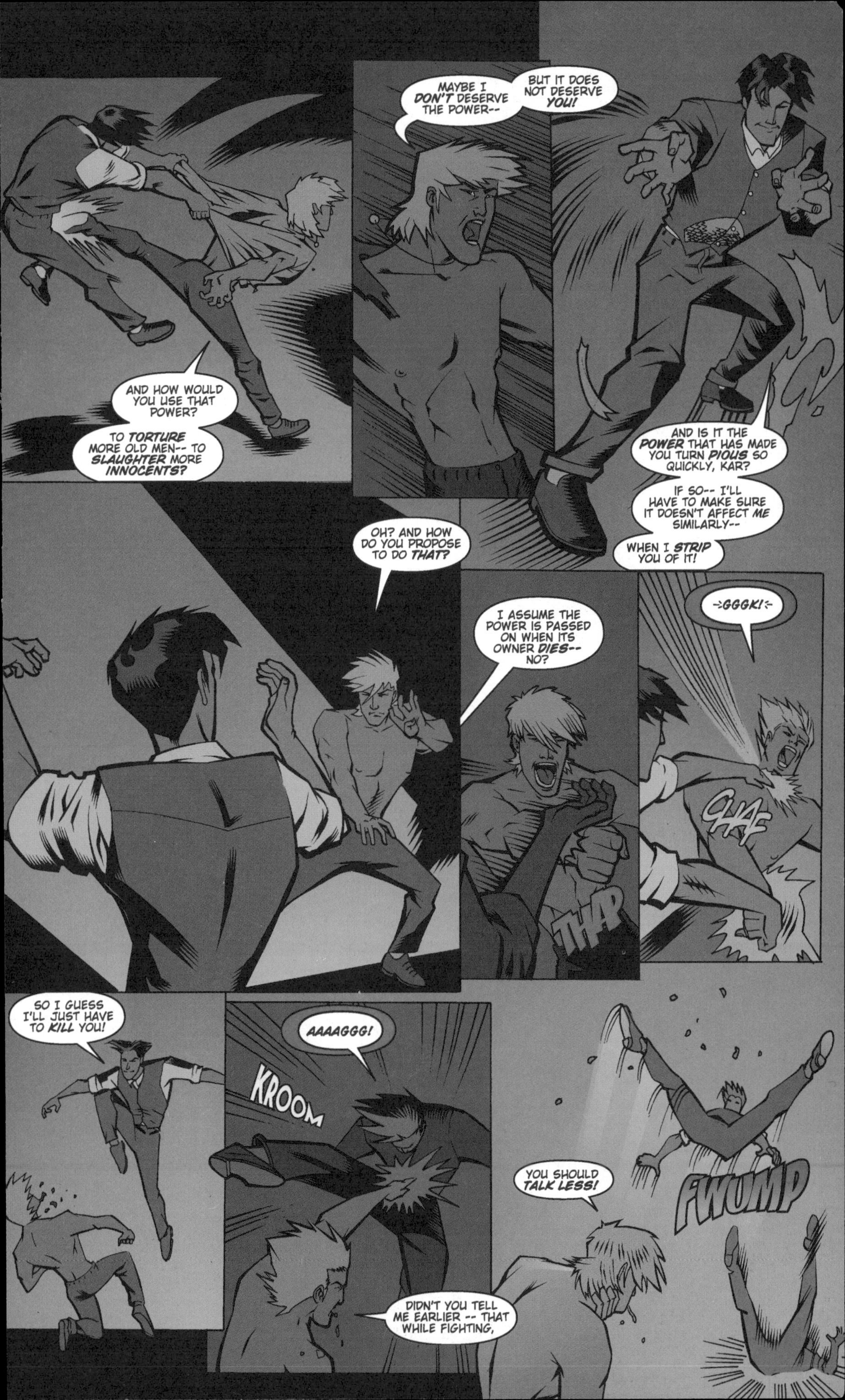
AND HOW WOULD YOU USE THAT POWER?
TO TORTURE MORE OLD MEN-- TO SLAUGHTER MORE INNOCENTS?
MAYBE I DON'T DESERVE THE POWER--
BUT IT DOES NOT DESERVE YOU!
AND IS IT THE POWER THAT HAS MADE YOU TURN PIOUS SO QUICKLY, KAR?
IF SO-- I'LL HAVE TO MAKE SURE IT DOESN'T AFFECT ME SIMILARLY--
WHEN I STRIP YOU OF IT!
OH? AND HOW DO YOU PROPOSE TO DO THAT?
I ASSUME THE POWER IS PASSED ON WHEN ITS OWNER DIES-- NO?
THAP
-GGGK!-
CHAF
SO I GUESS I'LL JUST HAVE TO KILL YOU!
AAAAGGG!
KROOM
DIDN'T YOU TELL ME EARLIER -- THAT WHILE FIGHTING,
YOU SHOULD TALK LESS!
FWUMP

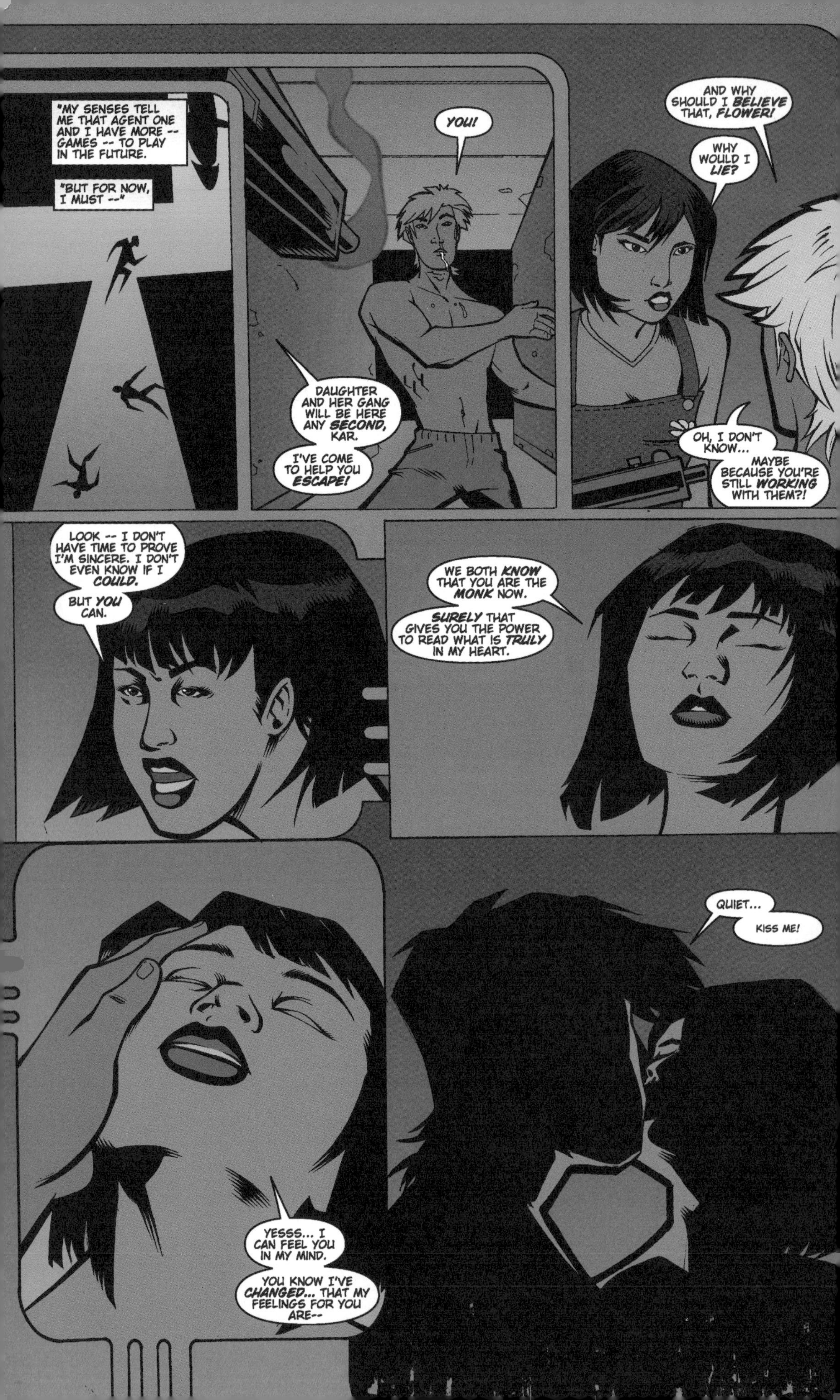
"MY SENSES TELL ME THAT AGENT ONE AND I HAVE MORE -- GAMES -- TO PLAY IN THE FUTURE.
"BUT FOR NOW, I MUST --"
YOU!
DAUGHTER AND HER GANG WILL BE HERE ANY SECOND, KAR.
I'VE COME TO HELP YOU ESCAPE!
AND WHY SHOULD I BELIEVE THAT, FLOWER!
WHY WOULD I LIE?
OH, I DON'T KNOW...
MAYBE BECAUSE YOU'RE STILL WORKING WITH THEM?!
LOOK -- I DON'T HAVE TIME TO PROVE I'M SINCERE. I DON'T EVEN KNOW IF I COULD.
BUT YOU CAN.
WE BOTH KNOW THAT YOU ARE THE MONK NOW.
SURELY THAT GIVES YOU THE POWER TO READ WHAT IS TRULY IN MY HEART.
YESSS... I CAN FEEL YOU IN MY MIND.
YOU KNOW I'VE CHANGED... THAT MY FEELINGS FOR YOU ARE--
QUIET...
KISS ME!

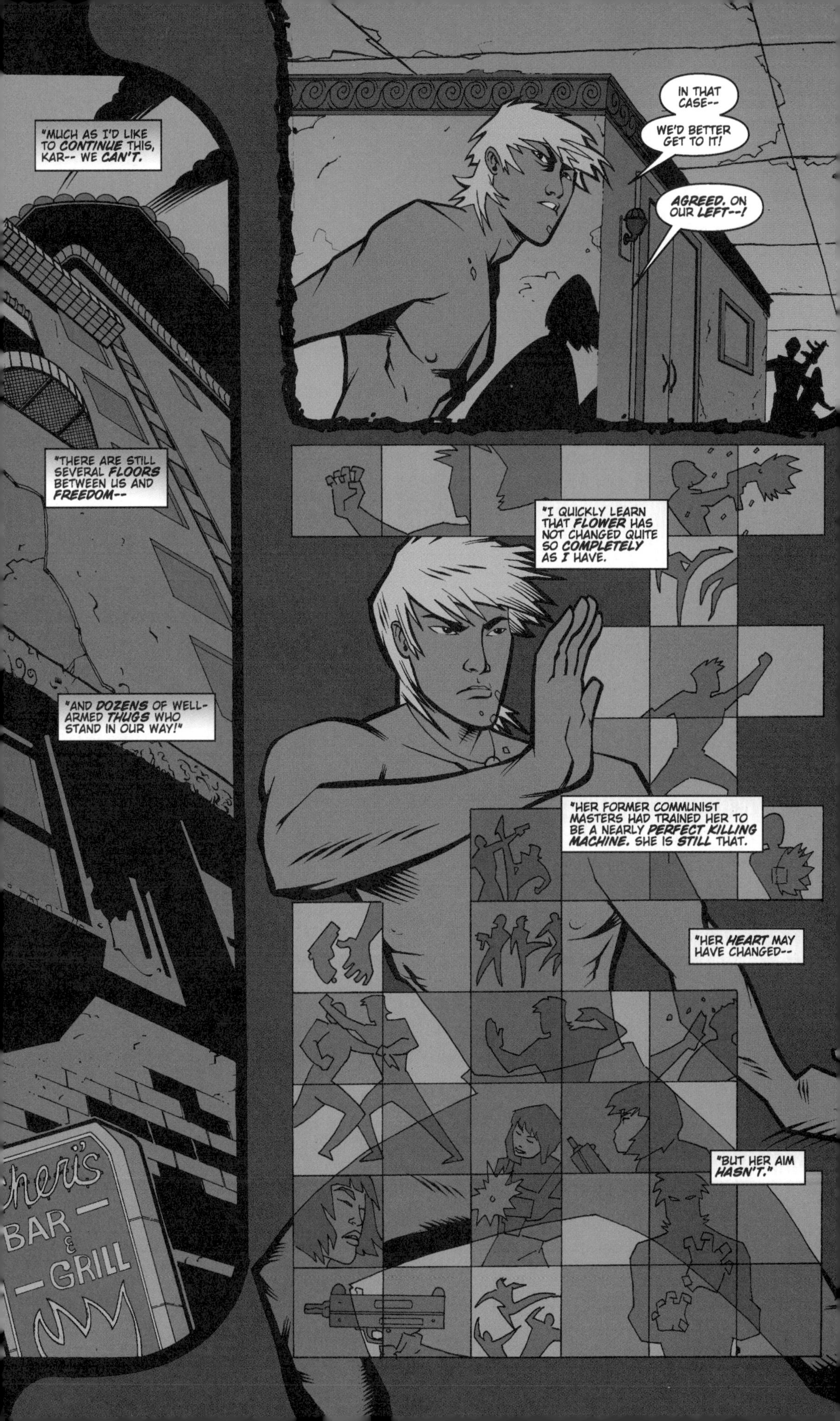
"MUCH AS I'D LIKE TO CONTINUE THIS, KAR-- WE CAN'T.
IN THAT CASE--
WE'D BETTER GET TO IT!
AGREED. ON OUR LEFT--!
"THERE ARE STILL SEVERAL FLOORS BETWEEN US AND FREEDOM--
"AND DOZENS OF WELL-ARMED THUGS WHO STAND IN OUR WAY!"
"I QUICKLY LEARN THAT FLOWER HAS NOT CHANGED QUITE SO COMPLETELY AS I HAVE.
"HER FORMER COMMUNIST MASTERS HAD TRAINED HER TO BE A NEARLY PERFECT KILLING MACHINE. SHE IS STILL THAT.
"HER HEART MAY HAVE CHANGED--
"BUT HER AIM HASN'T."
BAR & GRILL

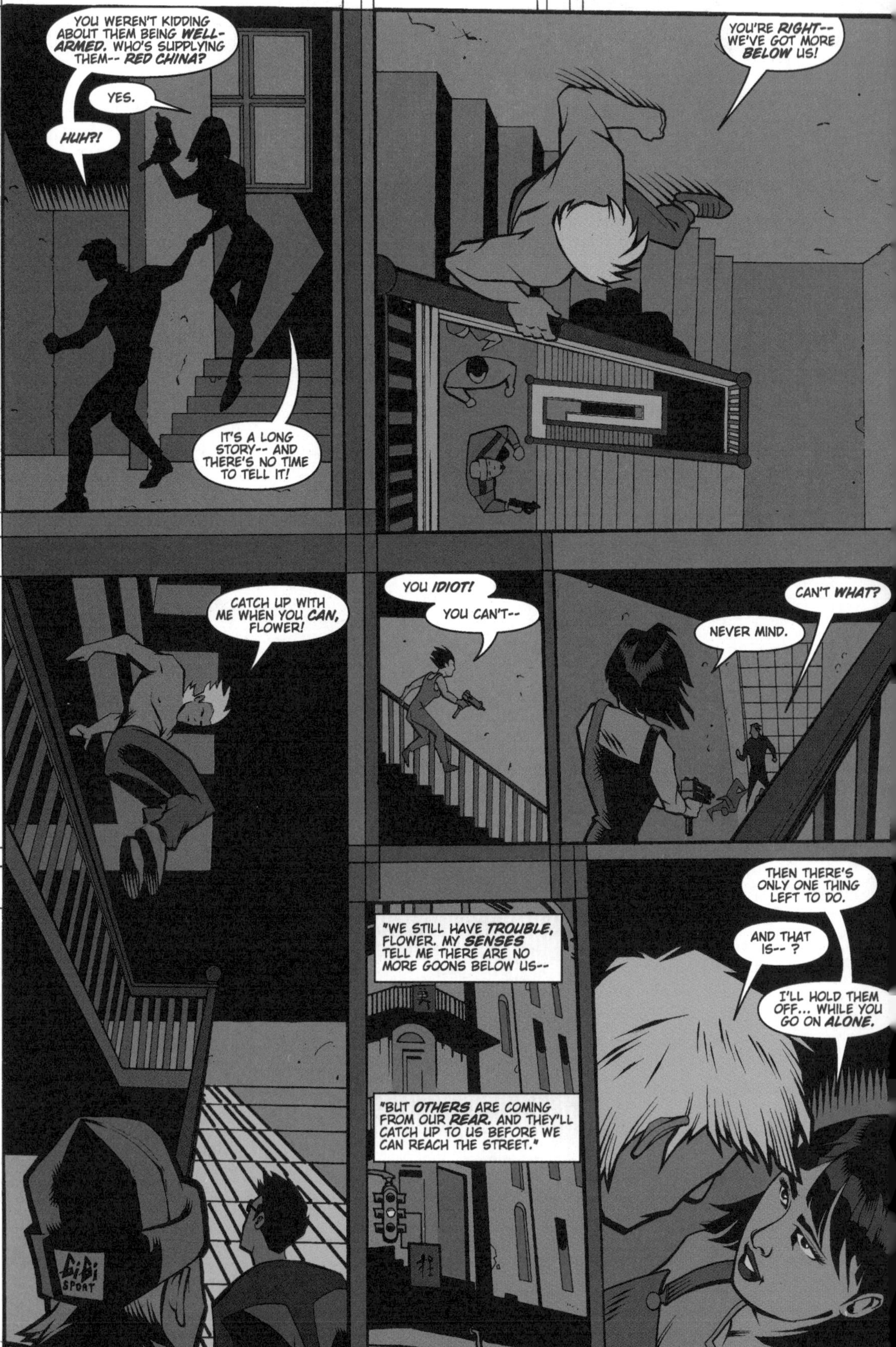
YOU WEREN'T KIDDING ABOUT THEM BEING WELL-ARMED. WHO'S SUPPLYING THEM-- RED CHINA?
YES.
HUH?!
IT'S A LONG STORY-- AND THERE'S NO TIME TO TELL IT!
YOU'RE RIGHT-- WE'VE GOT MORE BELOW US!
CATCH UP WITH ME WHEN YOU CAN, FLOWER!
YOU IDIOT!
YOU CAN'T--
CAN'T WHAT?
NEVER MIND.
"WE STILL HAVE TROUBLE, FLOWER. MY SENSES TELL ME THERE ARE NO MORE GOONS BELOW US--
"BUT OTHERS ARE COMING FROM OUR REAR. AND THEY'LL CATCH UP TO US BEFORE WE CAN REACH THE STREET."
THEN THERE'S ONLY ONE THING LEFT TO DO.
AND THAT IS-- ?
I'LL HOLD THEM OFF... WHILE YOU GO ON ALONE.
GiBi SPORT

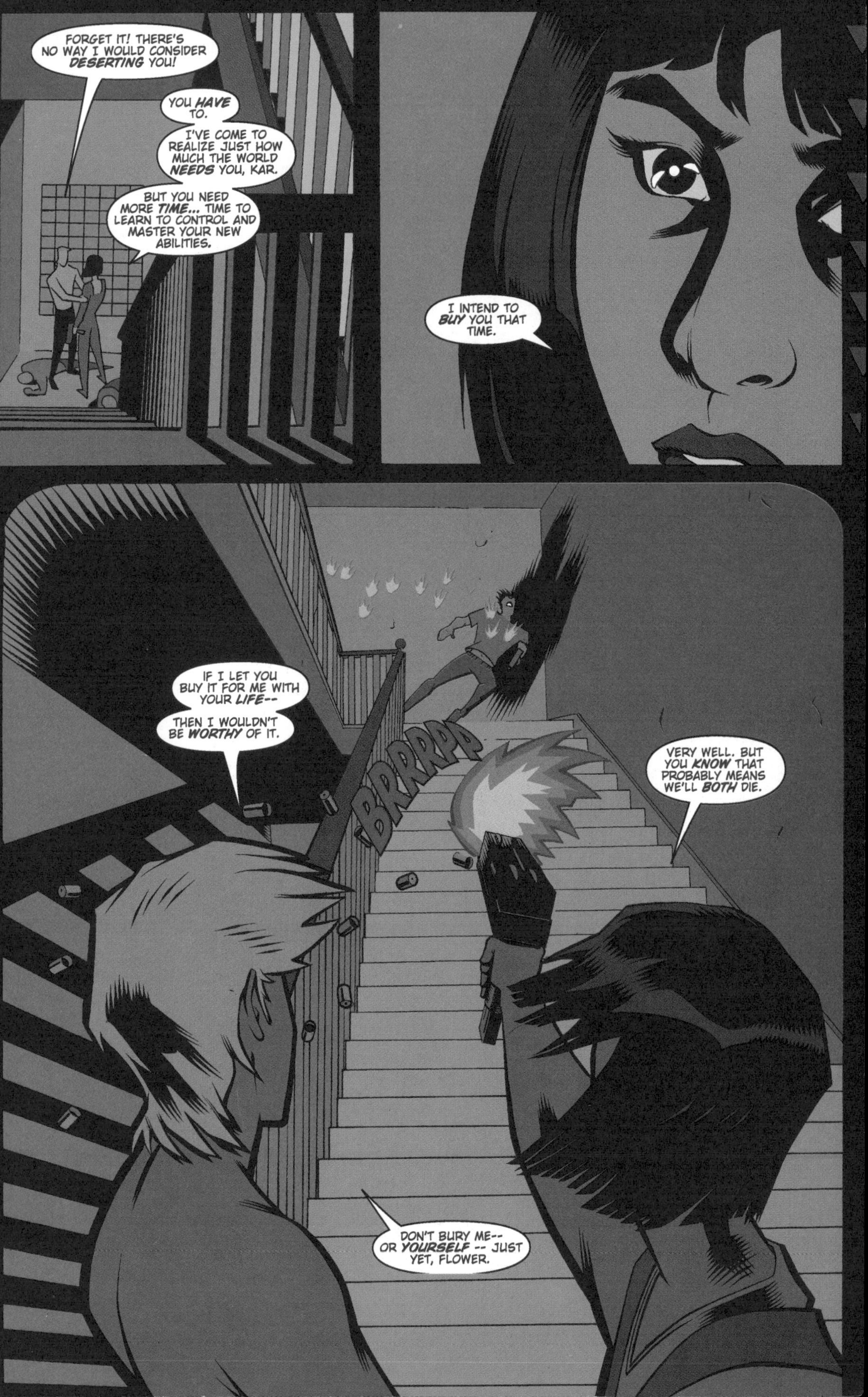
FORGET IT! THERE'S NO WAY I WOULD CONSIDER DESERTING YOU!
YOU HAVE TO.
I'VE COME TO REALIZE JUST HOW MUCH THE WORLD NEEDS YOU, KAR.
BUT YOU NEED MORE TIME... TIME TO LEARN TO CONTROL AND MASTER YOUR NEW ABILITIES.
I INTEND TO BUY YOU THAT TIME.
IF I LET YOU BUY IT FOR ME WITH YOUR LIFE--
THEN I WOULDN'T BE WORTHY OF IT.
BRRRPP
VERY WELL. BUT YOU KNOW THAT PROBABLY MEANS WE'LL BOTH DIE.
DON'T BURY ME-- OR YOURSELF -- JUST YET, FLOWER.

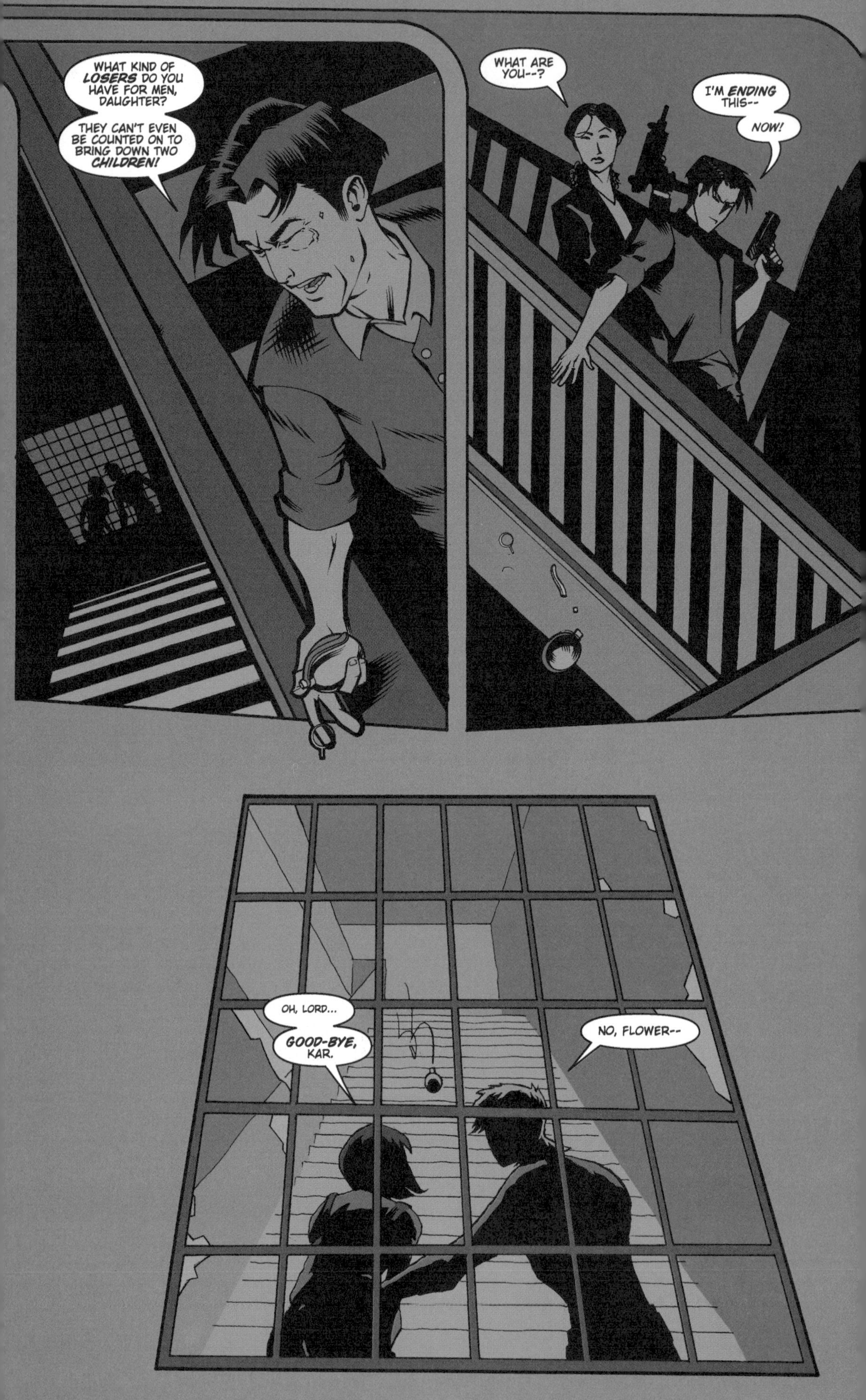
WHAT KIND OF LOSERS DO YOU HAVE FOR MEN, DAUGHTER?
THEY CAN'T EVEN BE COUNTED ON TO BRING DOWN TWO CHILDREN!
WHAT ARE YOU--?
I'M ENDING THIS--
NOW!
OH, LORD...
GOOD-BYE, KAR.
NO, FLOWER--

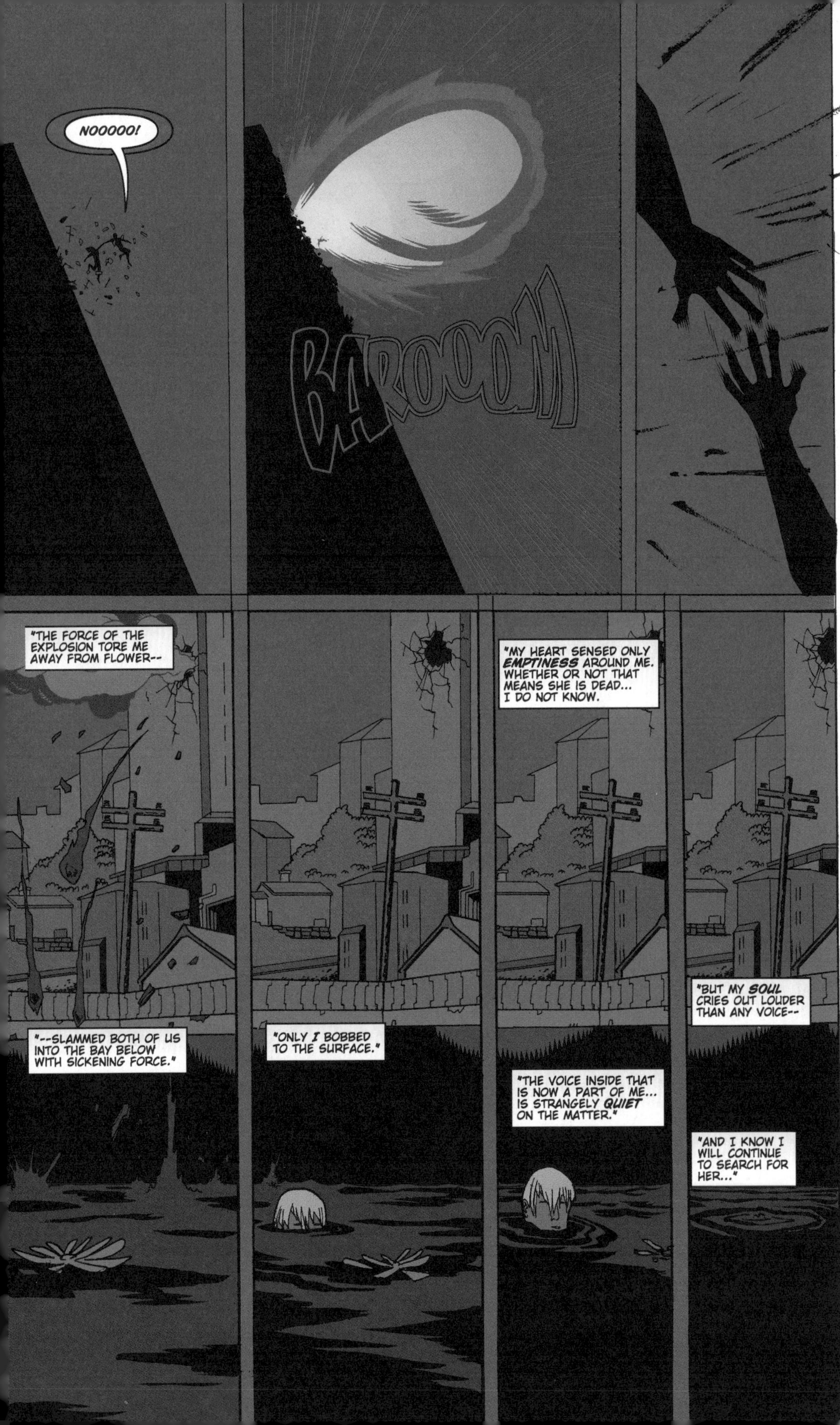
NOOOOO!
BAROOOM
"THE FORCE OF THE EXPLOSION TORE ME AWAY FROM FLOWER--
"--SLAMMED BOTH OF US INTO THE BAY BELOW WITH SICKENING FORCE."
"ONLY I BOBBED TO THE SURFACE."
"MY HEART SENSED ONLY EMPTINESS AROUND ME. WHETHER OR NOT THAT MEANS SHE IS DEAD... I DO NOT KNOW.
"THE VOICE INSIDE THAT IS NOW A PART OF ME... IS STRANGELY QUIET ON THE MATTER."
"BUT MY SOUL CRIES OUT LOUDER THAN ANY VOICE--
"AND I KNOW I WILL CONTINUE TO SEARCH FOR HER..."

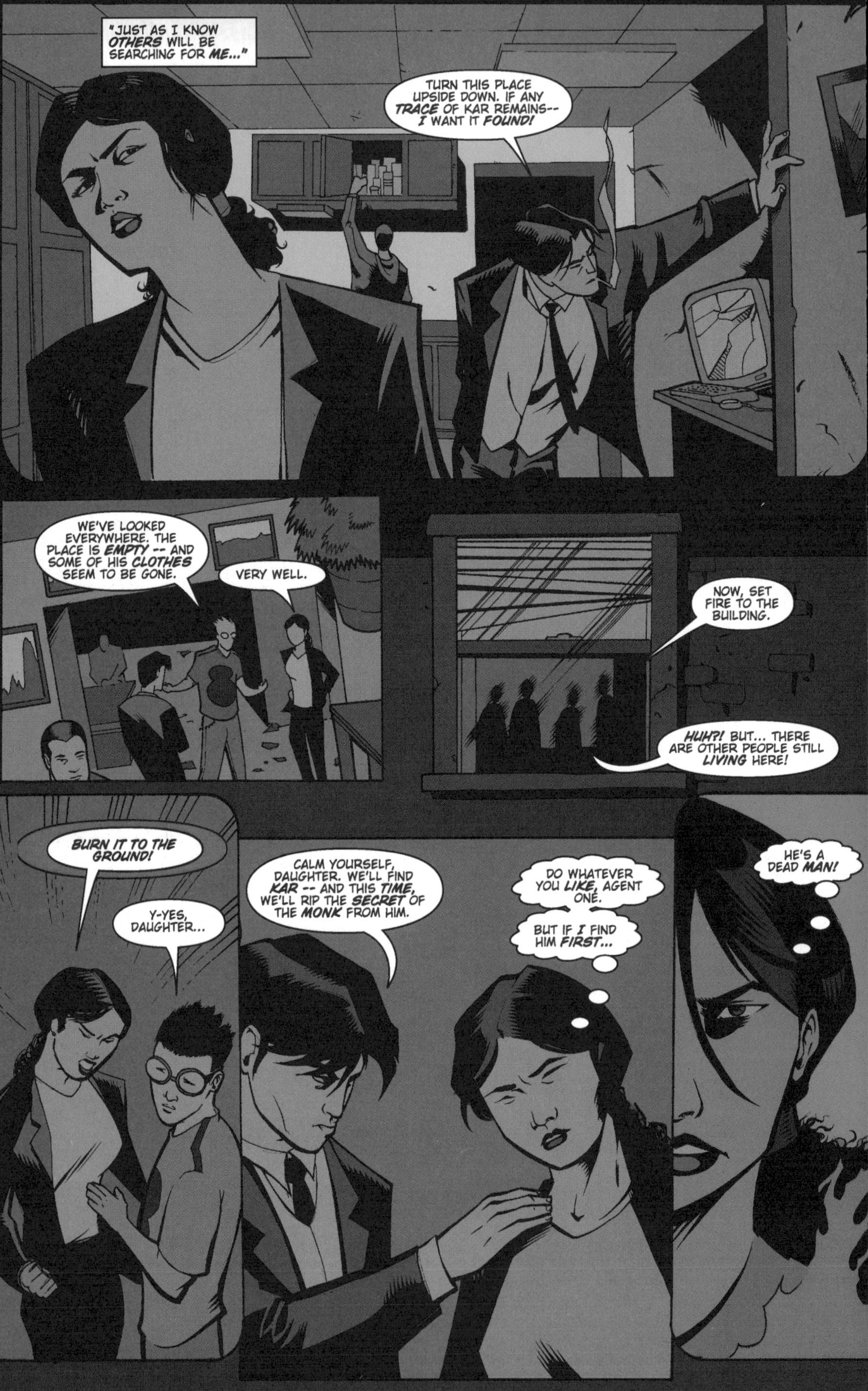
"JUST AS I KNOW OTHERS WILL BE SEARCHING FOR ME..."
TURN THIS PLACE UPSIDE DOWN. IF ANY TRACE OF KAR REMAINS-- I WANT IT FOUND!
WE'VE LOOKED EVERYWHERE. THE PLACE IS EMPTY -- AND SOME OF HIS CLOTHES SEEM TO BE GONE.
VERY WELL.
NOW, SET FIRE TO THE BUILDING.
HUH?! BUT... THERE ARE OTHER PEOPLE STILL LIVING HERE!
BURN IT TO THE GROUND!
Y-YES, DAUGHTER...
CALM YOURSELF, DAUGHTER. WE'LL FIND KAR -- AND THIS TIME, WE'LL RIP THE SECRET OF THE MONK FROM HIM.
DO WHATEVER YOU LIKE, AGENT ONE.
BUT IF I FIND HIM FIRST...
HE'S A DEAD MAN!

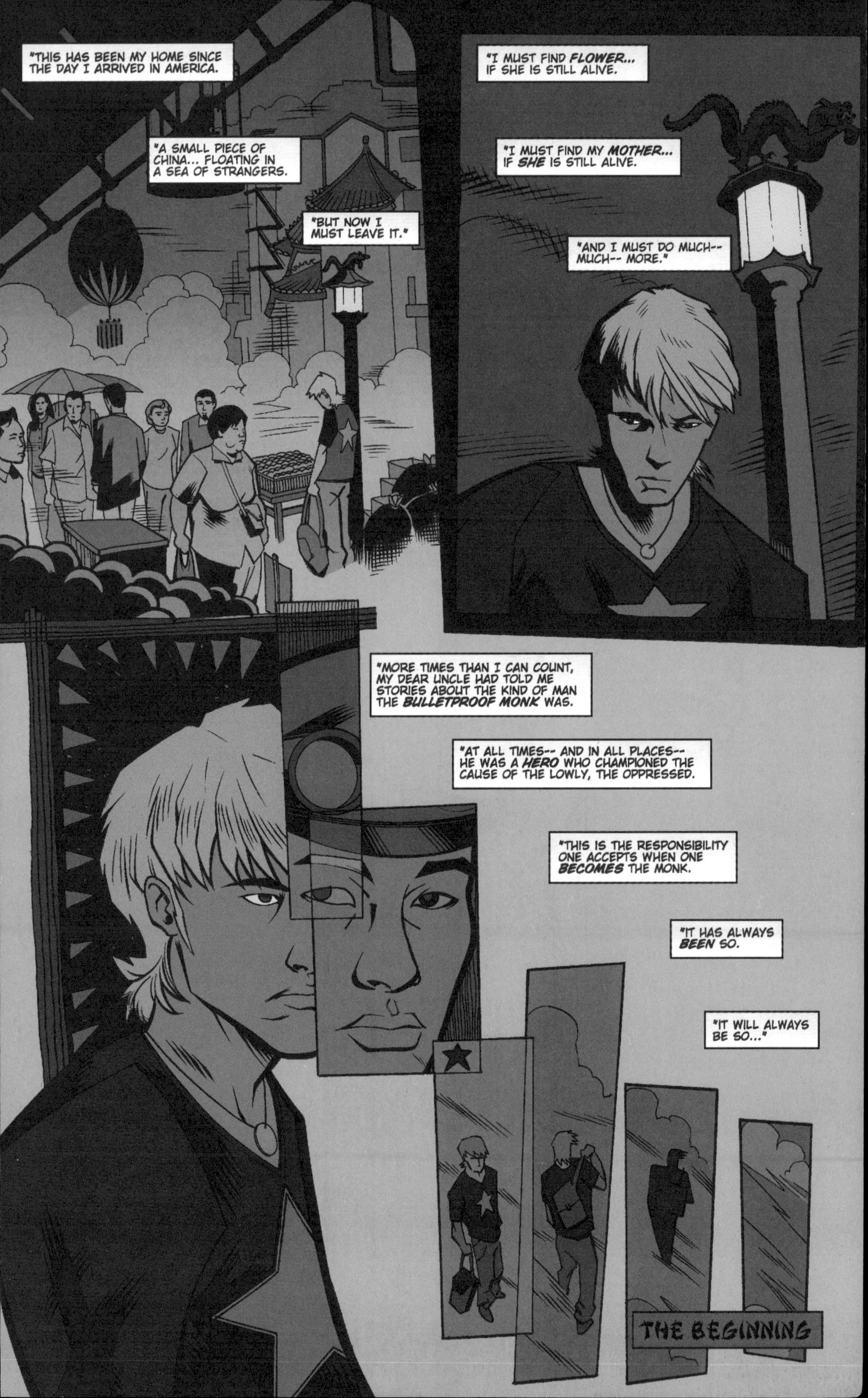
"THIS HAS BEEN MY HOME SINCE THE DAY I ARRIVED IN AMERICA.
"A SMALL PIECE OF CHINA... FLOATING IN A SEA OF STRANGERS.
"BUT NOW I MUST LEAVE IT."
"I MUST FIND FLOWER... IF SHE IS STILL ALIVE.
"I MUST FIND MY MOTHER... IF SHE IS STILL ALIVE.
"AND I MUST DO MUCH-- MUCH-- MORE."
"MORE TIMES THAN I CAN COUNT, MY DEAR UNCLE HAD TOLD ME STORIES ABOUT THE KIND OF MAN THE BULLETPROOF MONK WAS.
"AT ALL TIMES-- AND IN ALL PLACES-- HE WAS A HERO WHO CHAMPIONED THE CAUSE OF THE LOWLY, THE OPPRESSED.
"THIS IS THE RESPONSIBILITY ONE ACCEPTS WHEN ONE BECOMES THE MONK.
"IT HAS ALWAYS BEEN SO.
"IT WILL ALWAYS BE SO..."
THE BEGINNING

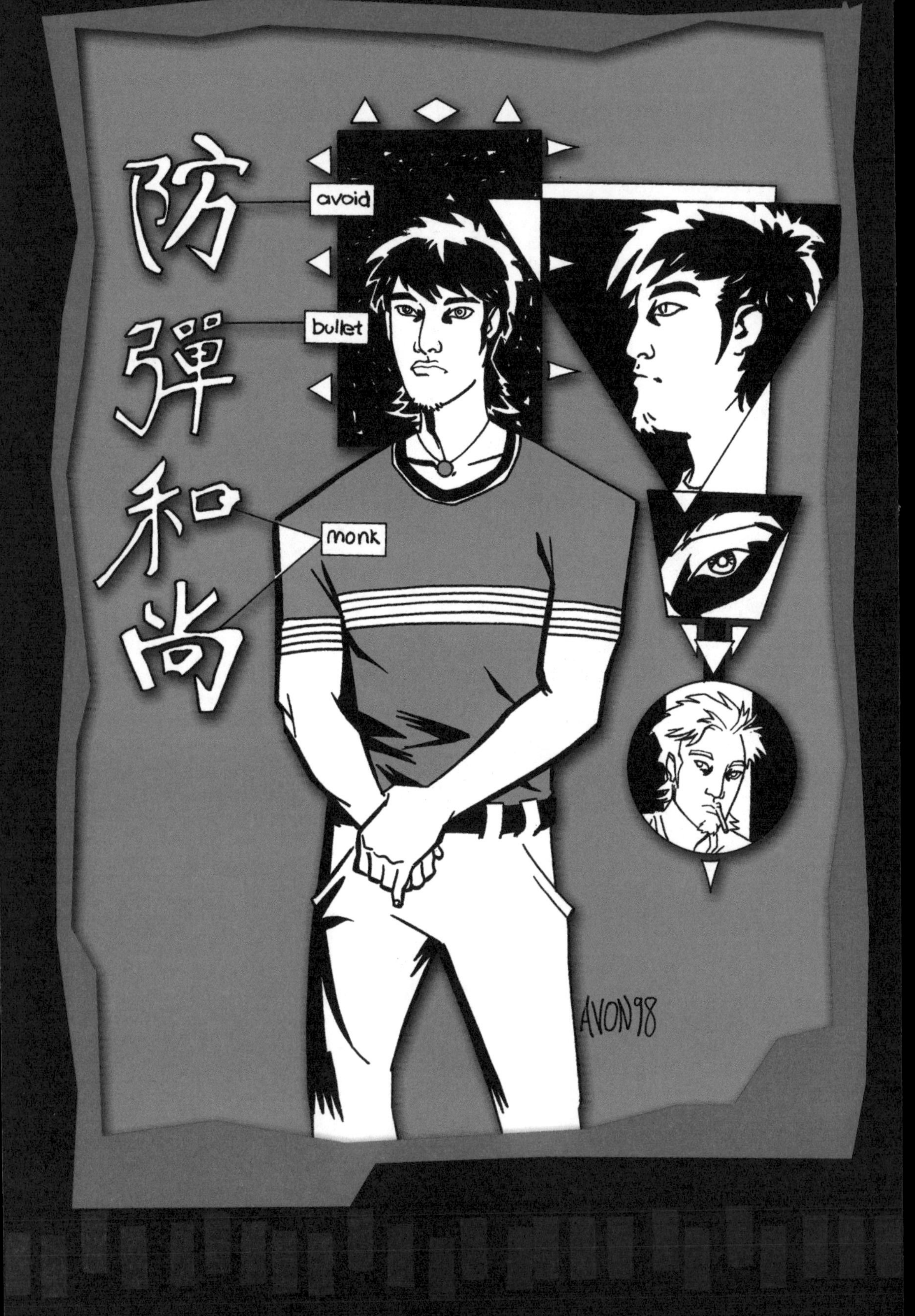
防
avoid
弾
bullet
和尚
monk
AVON98

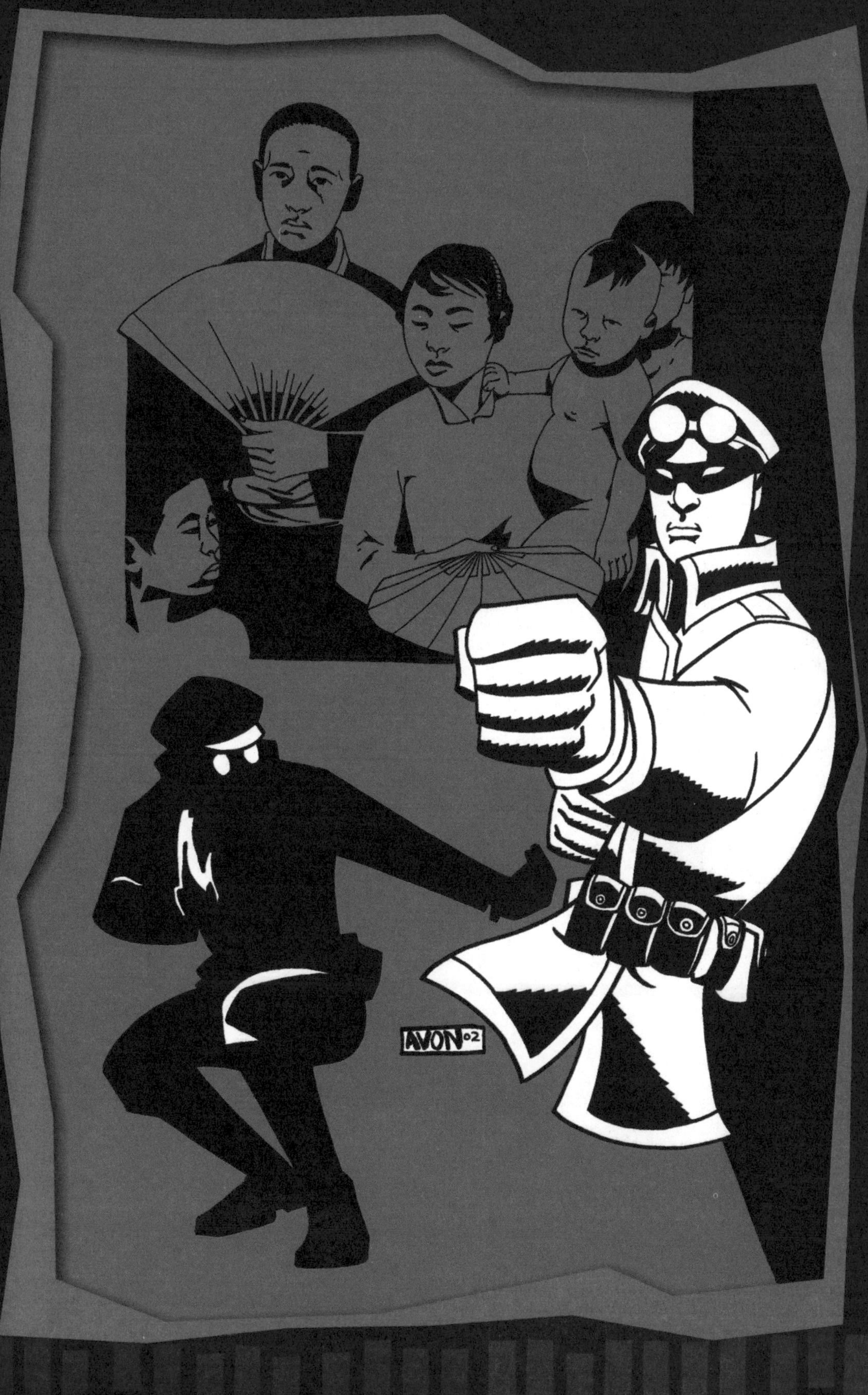
AVON 02

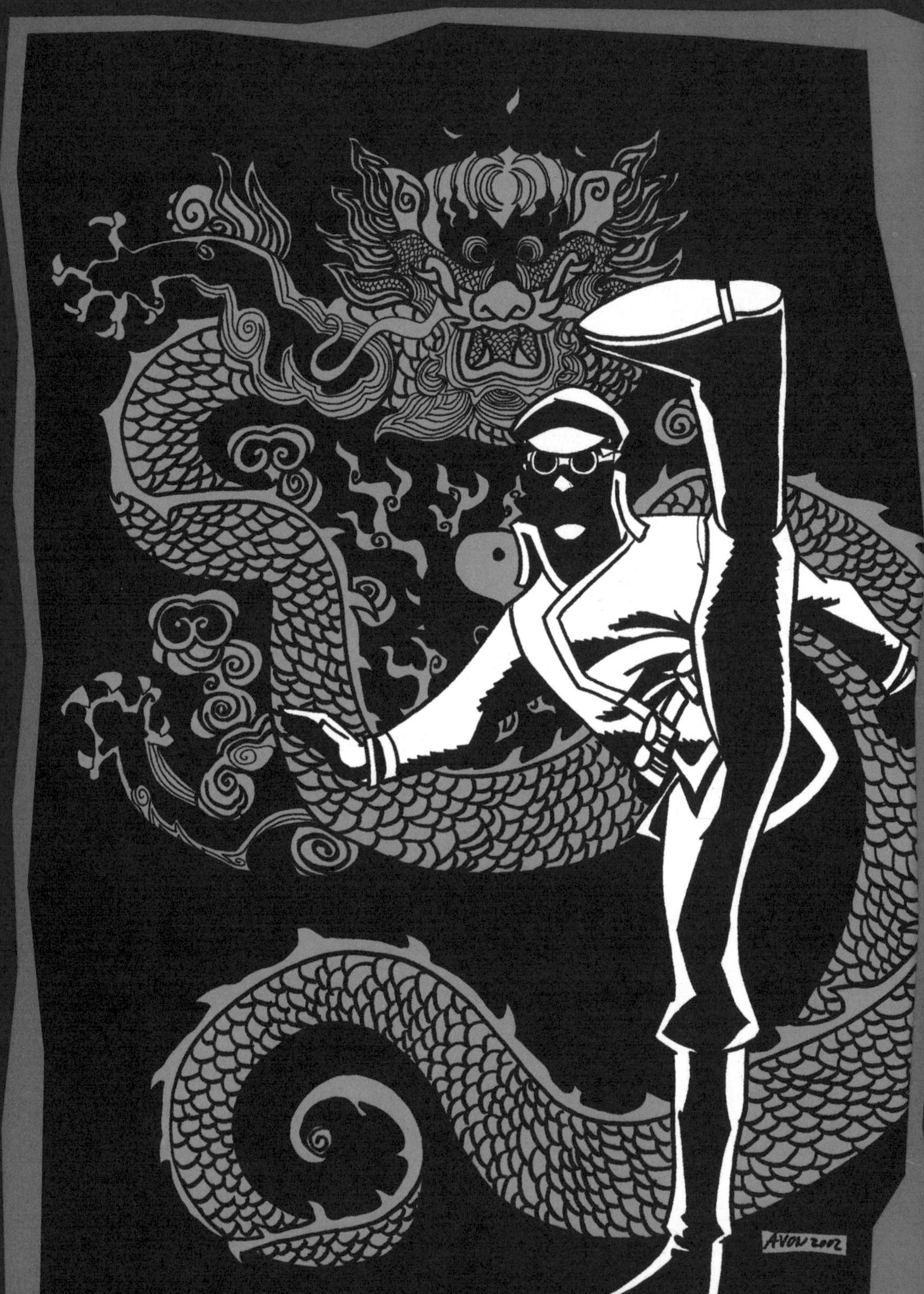
A.VON 2002

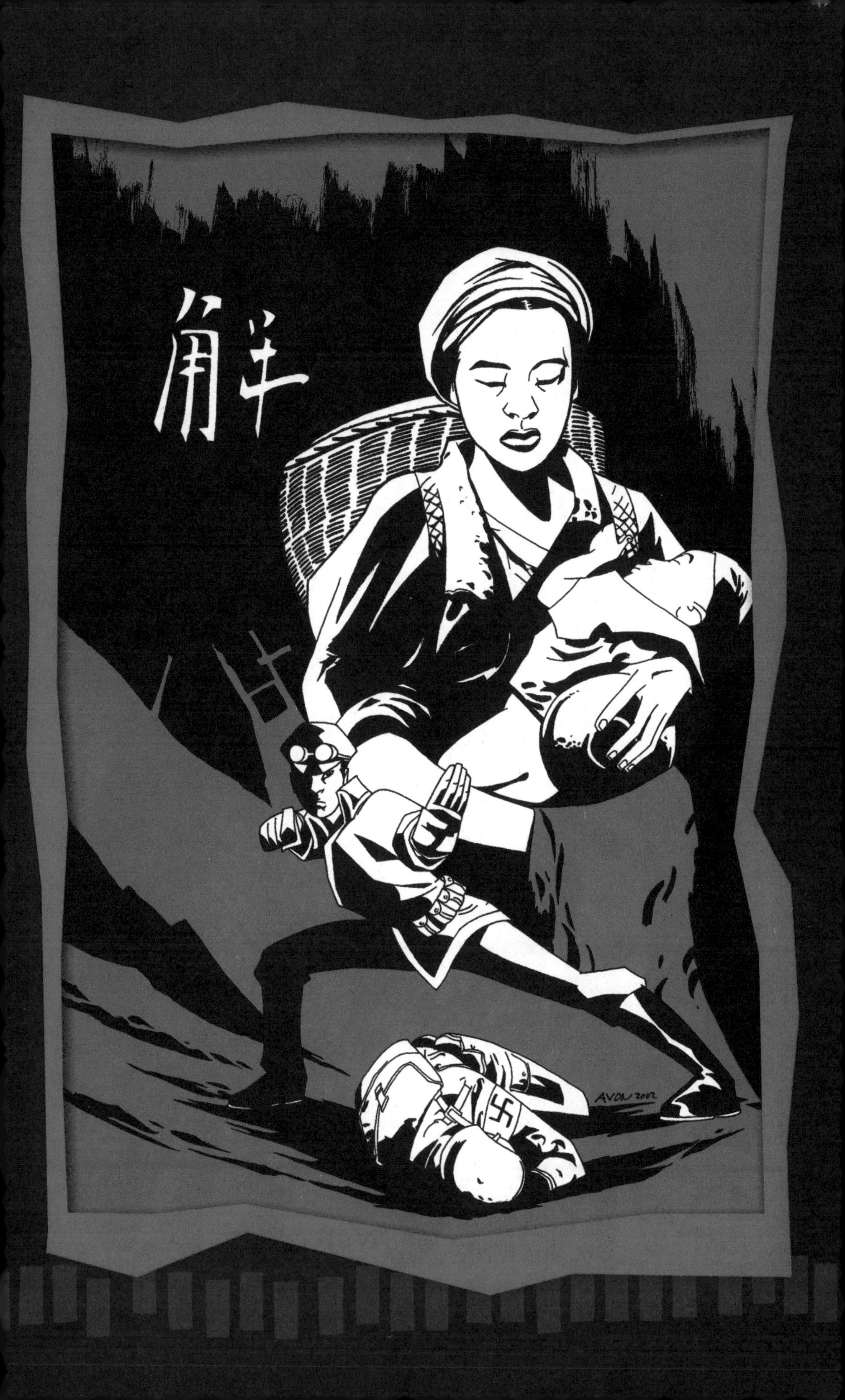
AVON 2002

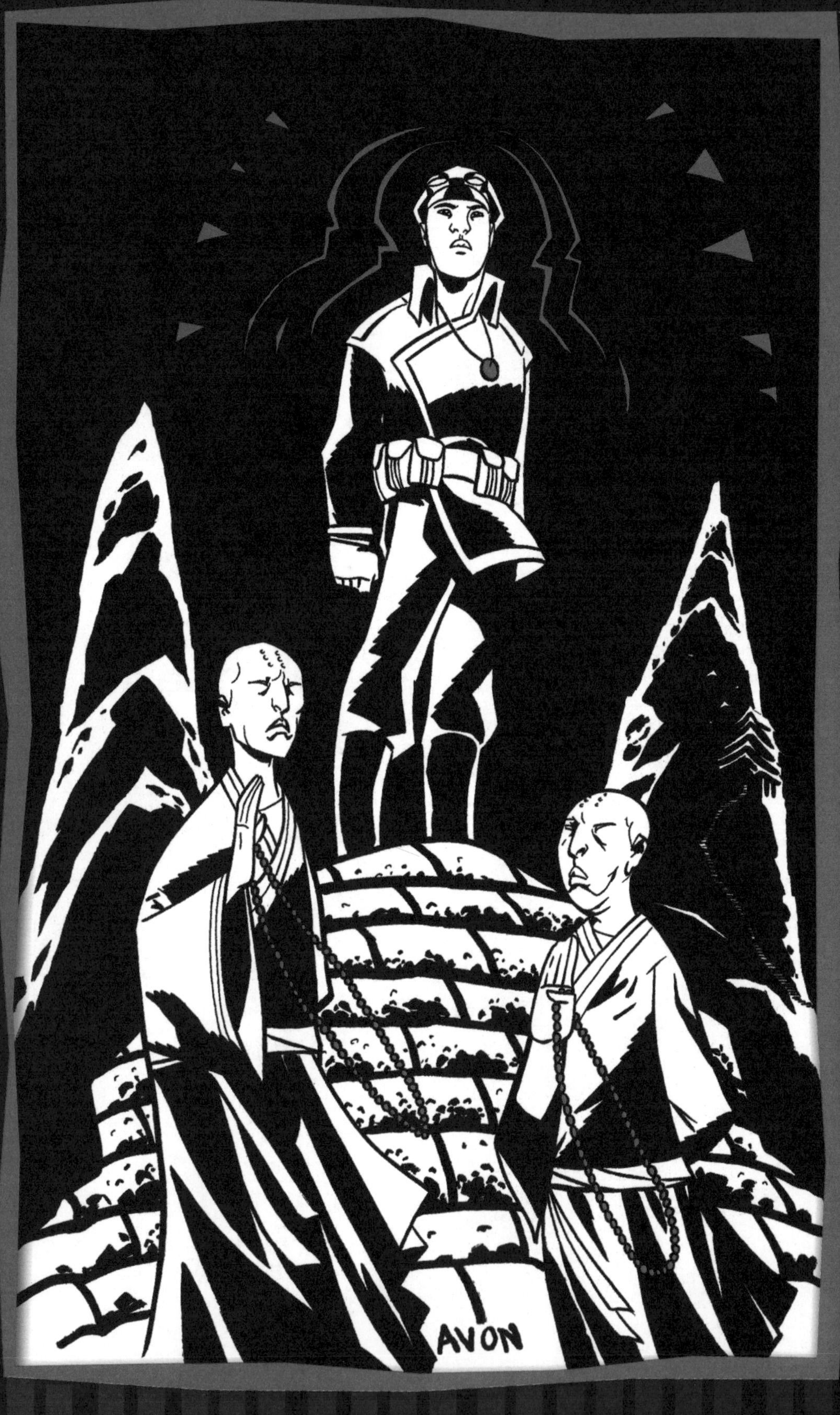
AVON

AVON 2012